The Search

A Young Person's Quest for Understanding

The author in 1950

The Search

A Young Person's Quest for Understanding

J. Donald Walters

Excerpted From *The Path*

Crystal Clarity, Publishers
14618 Tyler Foote Road
Nevada City, California 95959

Cover design by Bella Potapovskaya

Copyright © 1988 by J. Donald Walters
International Book Number 0-916124-46-0
Printed in the United States of America

Contents

1. The Pilgrim Whittles His Staff 7
2. He Sets Out from Home 14
3. Storm Clouds 30
4. A Temporary Haven 43
5. The Storm Breaks 52
6. A Paper Rest House: the "Popularity Game" 67
7. To Thine Own Search Be True 77
8. Joy Is the Goal 91
9. He Gathers Strength for the Climb 106
10. Intellectual Traps 124
11. By-Paths 133
12. "Who Am I? What Is God?" 143
13. A Search for Guide-Maps 166
14. Joy Is Inside! 175
15. A Map Discovered 186
16. The Pilgrim Meets His Guide 196

Other books by the same author:

Crises In Modern Thought
Rays of the Same Light
Cities of Light
The Artist as a Channel
The Art of Supportive Leadership
Education for Life

Chapter One

The Pilgrim Whittles His Staff

THERE ARE TIMES when a human being, though perhaps not remarkable in himself, encounters some extraordinary person or event that infuses his life with great meaning. My own life was blessed with such an encounter in 1948. Right here in America, of all lands the epitome of bustling efficiency, material progressiveness, and pragmatic "know-how," I met a great, God-known master whose constant vision was of eternity. His name was Paramhansa Yogananda. He was from India, though it would be truer to say that his home was the whole world.

Had anyone suggested to me prior to that meeting that so much radiance, dynamic joy, unaffected humility, and love might be found in a single human being, I would have replied — though perhaps with a sigh of regret — that such perfection is not possible for man. And had anyone suggested to me, further, that divine miracles have occurred in this scientific age, I would have laughed outright. For in those days, proud as I was in my intellectual, Twentieth-Century "wisdom," I mocked even the miracles of the Bible.

No longer. I have seen things that made a mockery of mockery itself. I know now from personal experience that divine wonders do occur on earth. And I believe that the time is approaching when countless men and women will no more think of doubting God than they doubt the air they breathe. For God is not dead. It is man only who dies to all that is wonderful in life when he limits himself to worldly acquisitions and to advancing himself in worldly eyes, but overlooks those spiritual realities which are the foundation of all that he truly *is*.

Paramhansa Yogananda often spoke of America's high spiritual destiny. When first I heard him do so, I marveled. *America?* All that I knew of this country was its materialism, its competitive drive, its smug, "no-nonsense" attitude toward anything too subtle to be measured with scientific instruments. But in time that great teacher made me aware of another aspect, an undercurrent of divine yearning, not in our intellectuals, perhaps, our so-called cultural "leaders," but in the hearts of the common people. Americans' love of freedom, after all, began in the quest, centuries ago, for *religious* freedom. Their historic emphasis on equality and on voluntary, friendly cooperation with one another reflects principles that are taught in the Bible. Americans' pioneering spirit is rooted in these principles. And when no frontiers remained to our people on the North American continent and they began exporting their pioneering energies abroad, again it was the spirit of freedom and of willing cooperation that they carried with them, setting a new example for mankind everywhere. In these twin principles Paramhansa Yogananda saw the key to mankind's next upward step in its evolution.

The vision of the future that he presented to us was of a state of world brotherhood in which all men would live together in harmony and freedom. As a step toward this universal fulfillment he urged those people who were free to do so to band together into what he called "world-brotherhood colonies": spiritual communities where people, living and working together with others of like mind, would develop an awareness of the true kinship of all men as sons and daughters of the same, one God.

It has been my own lot to found such a "world-brotherhood colony," the first of what Yogananda predicted would someday be thousands of such communities the world over.

Because the pioneering spirit is rooted in principles that are essentially spiritual, it has not only expanded men's frontiers outwardly; in recent decades especially, it has begun to *interiorize* them, to expand the inward boundaries of human consciousness, and to awaken in people the desire to harmonize their lives with truth, and with God.

It was to the divine aspirations of these pioneers of the spirit that Paramhansa Yogananda was responding in coming to America. Americans, he said, were ready to learn meditation and God-communion, through the practice of the ancient science of yoga.* It was in the capacity of one of modern India's greatest exponents of yoga that he was sent by his great teachers to the West.

In my own life and heritage, the pioneering spirit in all its stages of manifestation has played an important role. Numerous ancestors on both sides of my family were pioneers of the traditional sort, many of them ministers of the Gospel, and frontier doctors. My paternal grandparents joined the great land rush that opened up the Oklahoma Territory in 1889. Other ancestors played less exploratory, but nonetheless active, roles in the great adventure of America's development. Mary Todd, the wife of Abraham Lincoln, was a relative of mine. So also was Robert E. Lee, Lincoln's adversary in the Civil War. It pleases me thus to be linked with both sides of that divisive conflict, for my own lifelong tendency has been to reconcile contradictions — to seek, as India's philosophy puts it, "unity in diversity."

My father, Ray P. Walters, was born too late to be a pioneer in the earlier sense. A pioneer nevertheless at heart, he joined the new wave of international expansion and cooperation, working for Esso as an oil geologist in foreign lands. Mother, Gertrude G. Walters, was a part of this new wave also:

---

*Yoga: a Sanskrit word meaning, "union." Yoga is also a system of psycho-physical techniques for helping man to achieve conscious union with the Infinite Spirit, God. The yogi, a practitioner of the yoga science, acquires outwardly also a vision of the underlying unity of all life.

After graduating from college she went to study the violin in Paris. Both my parents were born in Oklahoma; it was in Paris, however, that they met. After their wedding, Dad was assigned to the oil fields of Rumania; there they settled in Teleajen, a small Anglo-American colony about three kilometers east of the city of Ploești. Teleajen was the scene of my own squalling entrance onto the stage of life.

My body, typically of the American "melting pot," is the product of a blend of several countries: England, Wales, Scotland, Ireland, Holland, France, and Germany. It was little Wales, the smallest of these seven, that gave me my surname, Walters. For Kriyananda is a monastic appellation that I acquired only in 1955, when I was initiated into the ancient Swami order of India.

The human body, through the process of birth, is a new creation. Not so the soul. I came into this world, I believe, already fully myself. I chose this particular family because I found it harmonious to my own nature, and felt that these were the parents who would best afford me the opportunities I needed for my own spiritual development. Grateful as I am to my parents for taking me in, a stranger, I feel less indebted to them for making me what I am. I have described them, their forebears, and the country from which they came to show the trends with which I chose to affiliate, for whatever good I might be able to accomplish for myself, and perhaps, also, for others.

For everyone in this world is a pilgrim. He comes alone, treads his chosen path for a time, then leaves once more solitarily. His is a sacred destination, always dimly suspected, though usually not consciously known. Whether deliberately or by blind instinct, directly or indirectly, what all men are truly seeking is Joy — Joy infinite, Joy eternal, Joy divine.

Most of us, alas, wander about in this world like pilgrims without a map. We imagine Joy's shrine to be wherever money is worshipped, or power, or fame, or good times. It is only after ceaseless roaming that, disappointed at last, we pause in silent self-appraisal. And then it is we discover, perhaps with a shock, that our goal was never distant from us at all — indeed, *never any farther away than our own selves!*

This path we walk has no fixed dimensions. It is either long or short, depending only on the purity of our intentions. It is the path Jesus described when he said, "The kingdom of God cometh not with observation: Neither shall they say, Lo here! or, lo there! for, behold, the kingdom of God is within you."* Walking this path, we yet walk it not, for the goal, being inward, is ours already. We have only to claim it as our own.

The principal purpose of this book is to help you, the reader, to make good that claim. I hope in these pages, among other things, to help you avoid a few of the mistakes I myself have made in the search. For a person's failures may sometimes be as instructive as his successes.

I was born in Teleajen on May 19, 1926, at approximately seven in the morning. James Donald Walters is the full name I received at christening in

*Luke 17:20,21.

the little Anglican church in Ploeşti. Owing to a plethora of Jameses in the community, I was always known by my second name, Donald, in which I was the namesake of a step-uncle, Donald Quarles, who later served as Secretary of the Air Force under President Eisenhower. James, too, was a family name, being the name of my maternal grandfather. It was my ultimate destiny, however, to renounce such family identities altogether in favor of a higher, spiritual one.

Mother has told me that throughout her pregnancy she was filled with an inward joy. "Lord," she prayed repeatedly, "this first child I give to Thee."

Her blessing may not have borne fruit as early as she had hoped. But bear fruit it did, gradually — one might almost say, relentlessly — over the years.

For mine is the story of one who did his best to live without God, but who — thank God — failed in the attempt.

Chapter Two

He Sets Out from Home

JOY HAS ALWAYS been my first love. I have longed to share it with others.

My clearest early memories all relate to a special kind of happiness, one that seemed to have little to do with the things around me, that at best only reflected them. A lingering impression is one of wonder to be in this world at all. What was I doing here? Intuitively I felt that there must be some higher reality — another world, perhaps, radiant, beautiful, and harmonious, in relation to which this one represented mere exile. Beautiful sounds and colors thrilled me almost to ecstasy. Sometimes I would cover a table down to the floor with a colorful American Indian blanket, then crawl inside and fairly drink in the luminous colors. At other times, gazing into the prism formed by the broad edge of a mirror on my mother's dressing table, I would imagine myself living in a world of rainbow-colored lights. Often also, at night, I would see myself absorbed in a radiant inner light, and my consciousness would seem to expand beyond the limits of my body.

"You were eager for knowledge," Mother tells me, "not a little willful, but keenly sympathetic to the misfortunes of others." Smiling playfully, she adds, "I used to read children's books to you. If the hero was in trouble, I would point pityingly to his picture. As I did so, your lips quivered. 'Poor *this!*' you exclaimed." Mother (naughty *this!*) found my response so amusing that she sometimes played on it by pointing tragically to the cheerful pictures as well — a miserable ploy which, she informs me, invariably succeeded.

As I grew older, my inner joy spilled over into an intense enthusiasm for life. Teleajen gave us many opportunities to be creative in our play. We were far removed from the modern world of frequent movies, circuses, and other contrived amusements. Television was, of course, unknown at that time even in America. As a community composed mostly of English and American families, we were remote even from the mainstream of Rumanian culture. Our parents taught us a few standard Anglo-American games, but for the most part we invented our own. Our backyards became transformed into adventure lands. A long stepladder laid sideways on the snow became an airplane soaring us to warmer climes. A large apple tree with hanging branches served a variety of useful functions: a schoolhouse, a seagoing schooner, a castle. Furniture piled high in various ways in the nursery would become a Spanish galleon, or a mountain fortress. We blazed secret trails through a nearby cornfield to a cache of buried treasure, or to a point of safety from the pursuing officers of some unspeakably wicked tyrant. In winter, skating on a tennis court that had been flooded to make an ice rink, we gazed below us into the frozen depths and imagined ourselves moving freely in another dimension of wonderful shapes and colors.

I remember a ship, too, that I set out to build, fully intending to sail it on Lake Snagov. I got as far as nailing a few old boards together in nondescript imitation of a deck. In imagination, however, as I lay in bed at night and contemplated the job, I was already sailing my schooner on the high seas.

Leadership came naturally to me, though I was unwilling to exert it if others didn't share my interests spontaneously. The children in Teleajen did share them, and accepted my leadership. More and more, however, as I grew older, I discovered that people often considered my vision of things somewhat peculiar. I noticed it first in some of the newly arrived children in Teleajen. Accustomed to the standard childhood games of England and America, they would look puzzled at my proposals for more imaginative entertainment — like the time we gazed into unfamiliar dimensions in the ice while skating over it. Unwilling to impose my interests on others, I was equally unwilling to accept their imposition in return. I was, I suppose, a nonconformist, not from conscious desire or intent, but from a certain inability to attune myself to others' norms. What was important to me seemed to them unimportant, whereas, frequently, what they considered important seemed to me incomprehensible.

Miss Barbara Henson (now Mrs. Elsdale), our governess for a time, described me in a recent letter the way she remembers me as a child of seven: "You were certainly 'different,' Don — 'in the family but not of it.' I was always conscious that you had a mystic quality which set you apart, and others were aware of it, too. You were always the observer, with an extraordinarily straight look in those blue-grey eyes which made you, in a sense, ageless. And in a quiet, disconcerting way, you made funny little experiments on other people as if to satisfy your suspicions about something concerning them. Never to be put off by prevarication or half-truths, you were, one felt, seeking the truth behind everything."

Cora Brazier, our next-door neighbor, a kind, sympathetic lady, once remarked to Miss Henson, "I always try to be especially nice to Don, because he's not like the others. I believe he knows this, and is lonely."

Although this knowledge was not to dawn on me fully until after I left Teleajen, there was even there a certain sense of being alone. It was held in abeyance, however, by the presence of good friends, and by a harmonious home life.

My parents loved us children deeply. Their love for each other, too, was exemplary, and a strong source of emotional security for us. Never in my life have I known them to quarrel, or to have even the slightest falling out.

The Search

My father was especially wonderful with children. Rather reserved by nature, he yet possessed a simple kindness and a sense of humor that enabled him to appreciate young minds. At bedtime he would invent hilarious stories for us that were continued night after night, frequently with additions from his enthusiastic listeners. Then, as my brothers and I were ready to fall asleep, he would arrange us at one end of the bed or the other depending on whether we said we wanted to travel in sleep to Australia, America, or to some other distant land.

He taught us much, by example as well as words. Above all what we learned from him came from observing in him a nature always humble, honest, truthful, honorable, kind, and scrupulously fair. I would go so far as to call him, in his quiet, rather shy way, a great man.

But in my own relationship with him there was always a certain sadness. I could not be to him the kind of mirror a man naturally hopes for in his sons, especially in his first-born. I tried earnestly to share his interests, but where he was attracted to the "hows" of things, I was attracted to the "whys." He was a scientist, and I, instinctively, a philosopher. He tried to interest me in the way things worked. (I still remember a dusty expedition under the house, where he showed us boys what made the front doorbell ring. I at least *tried* to feel grateful!) But I was only interested in what things meant. My inability to communicate with him on those subjects which interested each of us most deeply was the first indication I had that his world — which I considered, by extension, the normal world — could never truly be mine.

Mother and I understood each other intuitively; ours was a communication of souls, less so of speech. Though she never spoke of praying for us children, I know that her prayers and love for me were my greatest blessing during the formative years of my life.

Rumania was still a feudal land. Its people, gifted artistically, tended otherwise to be somewhat inefficient and unhurried. The country was an anachronism in this busy Twentieth Century. Its workmen could spend fifteen years with picks and shovels digging a tunnel under the railway tracks at the main station in the capital. One summer, eager to follow the example of the rest of the modern world, the whole nation went on Daylight *Losing* Time, by official mistake! Drivers' tests included such penetrating questions as, "What goes on the front of a car?" (Headlights, naturally.) Years later, Indra Devi, the well-known yoga teacher,* told me that while traveling by train through Rumania she had once been asked by the conductor what she was doing in a second-class compartment.

"Why, can't you see? I have a second-class ticket!"

"Oh, that doesn't matter in *Rumania!* Please, just go sit in first class where everyone else is."

Inattention, however, to the petty details of modern commerce and efficiency seemed somehow appropriate in a land that inspired thoughts of music and poetry. Rumania was one of the most fascinatingly beautiful countries I have ever seen: a land

*Author of *Forever Young, Forever Healthy,* and other books.

of fertile plains and soaring mountains, of colorfully clad peasants and musically gifted gypsies, of hay carts on the highways vying with automobiles for the right of way, of giggling, naked children, of gay songs and laughter. Frequently, outside our colony in the evenings, we would hear bands of gypsies conversing, singing, or playing the violin: the sad, haunting melodies of a people forever outcast from their true home, in India. These gypsies were my first contact with the subtly subjective moods of the Orient — moods that, I was to learn, are reflected in many aspects of life in Rumania. For centuries Rumania had been under Turkish rule. Now a proud and upcoming Western nation, there still clung to her something of the aura of the mystical East.

Rumania was a kingdom. King Carol II had his summer home about sixty kilometers (forty miles) northwest of us, in Sinaia, a lovely hill station in the Transylvanian Alps. Though I never saw him there, we, too, spent many vacations in Sinaia, and in other quaint towns and villages nearby: Buşteni, Predeal, Timiş, Braşov. In winter we often skied; in summer we hiked, or waded and swam in friendly, chuckling brooks, or played in fragrant meadows. Many times these mountain trips were taken because of my health, which was precarious. I was skinny as a pencil, and forever coming down with a variety of obscure ailments. Timiş was my favorite spot. There we always stayed at a guest lodge run by a German lady, Frau Weidi, whose husband kept bees that produced the best honey I have ever eaten.

Sixty kilometers to the south of Teleajen was

He Sets Out from Home

Bucharest, Rumania's capital: a clean, modern city that rose like a prophetic dream in the mind of a nation still asleep in the Middle Ages. Ploeşti remained for me, however, the Big City for the first nine years of my life: a not-very-attractive jumble of dirty streets and uninteresting houses. My recollections of it are few: visits to Ghiculescu, the grocer; Sunday services at the Anglican church; and very occasional outings to the movies — Walt Disney cartoons, mostly, and comedies featuring Laurel and Hardy, whom the Rumanians had renamed fondly, Stan and Bran.

The church served as a focus for Mother's piety. In this area of her life Dad played the role of disinterested spectator. Though he respected Mother's religious inclinations, and went with her to church more or less regularly, I never observed that liturgy held any attraction for him. His own natural concept of reality was more abstract. Nothing, I think, so inspired him as the contemplation of vast eons of geologic time. The thought of a God sitting somewhere on a heavenly throne, bestowing favors on special groups of worshippers, struck him, I suspect, as faintly barbaric.

My own natural bent lay somewhere between these two, the pious and the abstract. Like Dad, I was not greatly attracted to the church worship services. The hymns seemed to me rather dull and sad. The minister I considered a good man, but certainly not an inspired one. I suppose I accepted the rituals as good things to do; beyond this pale recognition, however, they held little meaning for me. I wish I could report that the life of Jesus at least made a strong impression on me. I am moved by it now. But then it reached me through a filter of wooden traditionalism, robbed of immediacy. I'm sure I couldn't have defined my feelings at the time, but I think what I missed most of all in our church services were love and joy. Mother had these qualities. What impressed and touched me about her was not religion as she defined it, but as she lived it.

Like Dad, I found it difficult to believe in a God who loved each human being personally. That God was impersonal seemed to me self-evident, when I considered the vastness of the universe. How then, I thought, could He be interested enough to listen to us mortals when we prayed? It was only many years later, in the teachings of India, that I found reconciliation for these seemingly incompatible concepts of a God both personal and impersonal. For the Infinite Spirit, as my guru was to explain with perfect simplicity, though impersonal in its vastness, has become personal also, in creating individual beings. Infinity, in other words, implies infinitesimal littleness as well as infinite immensity.

Though I found it difficult to address God personally, I always felt that reality must be *spiritual*, that it must have some high meaning and purpose. I remember a discussion I had once with Dad. I was about six years old at the time; we were standing on the terrace of our Teleajen home, watching the birds at play in the large apple tree.

"In the hundreds of millions of years," Dad said, "since the world was created, every species has had its turn at being the master of this planet, except the birds. First there were the fishes, then the insects, then reptiles, and now man, who represents the mammals. Perhaps, millions of years from now, man, too, will be pushed aside, and the birds will get their turn at being the earth's masters."

How appealing I found this picture of the vast reaches of time! But then a doubt occurred to me: Is there no *meaning* to it all? Is life nothing but a process of endless change, with different species ruling for no better reason than that their turn has come? Surely there must be some higher purpose — hidden, perhaps, but divine.

My questioning mind must have made me something of a trial to my parents. Mother, on a visit to Italy in 1933, wrote to Miss Henson: "Please tell the boys that I want them to try to be very good and that will help both them and me to have a good time. (Donald is sure to find a flaw in that argument, but you might try it!)"

Fortunately for me, Mother and Dad never discouraged my questioning. I remember one day, at the age of five, standing in the bathroom, watching Dad shave. I was pondering one of the profound mysteries of childhood: How can Santa Claus reach every home in the world in a single night? Suddenly the answer dawned on me.

"Daddy, there isn't really a Santa Claus, is there?"

Dad, too honest to insist there is, but too considerate of the sweet myths of childhood to admit that there isn't, hedged his reply. I understood him perfectly. Then and there I decided that it really would be much nicer to go on believing in Santa Claus anyway. In that spirit I believe in him still.

The Search

Myths are an important part of life. Paradoxical as it seems, they are important to man's search for reality as well, for they help to give his mind the elasticity it needs to imagine new solutions to old problems.

Myths (in fact!) formed a large part of my education. I loved Greek mythology, the adventures of King Arthur and his knights of the Round Table, the legends of Robin Hood and Peter Pan, Grimm's fairy tales, stories from the Old Testament — myths, all, in which goodness, courage, and honor win in the end. One's life experiences may not always endorse such moral preachments, but wise men and women have ever insisted that justice does prevail, eventually, even if the time of reckoning stretches far beyond man's present horizons. "*Yato dharma, tato jaya,*" say the Indian Scriptures: "Where there is righteousness, there is victory." Fact may well, as people claim, be stranger than fiction, but fiction very often is, in a deeper sense, truer than fact. I think it a pity that the ancient myths are not given more emphasis in modern education. Certainly they enriched my own upbringing.

But then, the culture of Rumania was more conducive than pragmatic America's to the art of legend-telling. As children, my brothers and I got periodic opportunities to compare these two countries. Every three or four years Dad received a three-months' vacation, all expenses paid, in America. My first journey here was when I was six months old, then three years, seven, ten, and thirteen. It was after I turned thirteen that we settled here.

I still recall my amazement, at the age of three,

on reaching London and finding waiters, taxi drivers, the man in the street — all speaking English! I'd supposed English was spoken only by parents and their friends. Nurses, of course, spoke German, but wasn't it a law of life that practically everyone else spoke Rumanian? I suppose by so compartmentalizing these languages I managed to keep from confusing them — a further example, perhaps, of the value of the myth-making process. Once Mother addressed me in Rumanian, and I replied in shocked tones, "Mother, don't talk to me like that!"

Looking at America with eyes that were partly Rumanian, I gained insights that sometimes conflicted with my pride in being an American. I deeply loved America. I admired its dynamic energy, and stood almost in awe of its constant emphasis on common sense: The Americans I met seemed to know exactly what to do in every situation. I loved them, too, for their kindness — whenever they took the time from constant, driving activity to be kind. But on the other hand, I found myself puzzled by what often struck me in their conversation as "big talk." I'd noticed it in a few of the Americans in Teleajen, especially in the newcomers. In America even the children, it seemed, were always trying to demonstrate how grown-up they were, how sophisticated, how important. It was as though they had no patience with childhood. What, I wondered, was all that *important* about being important?

Compared to America, Rumania is a little country. Though independent in spirit, its people have a less exalted image of themselves. Americans, with their four million territorial square miles, fall more easily a prey to the thought of self-importance, a temptation which seems to accompany bigness whether in nations, institutions, or individuals.

Vacations in America entailed visits to our various relatives. My earliest memories include Mother Ella, my maternal grandmother, who died while I was still young. I remember best her sweet smile, so loving it seemed almost saintly. My paternal grandparents, who lived longer, were simple, good people too. It was in these relatives, and in many other people like them, that I caught my first glimpse of the particular spiritual genius of America: childlike innocence and simplicity, a predisposition to see goodness in others, a love of freedom tempered by a desire to live in harmony with man and God.

Grandad introduced me also to another American trait: the tendency to dignify inconsequential matters, humorously, by pretending that more serious issues are at stake. It is a trait that can, and sometimes does, lead to misunderstandings.

Once in Tulsa Dad paid a minor traffic fine. Grandad remarked to me afterwards, straight-facedly, "Well, I guess your Dad escaped prison this time." I took him literally. Several days later we were eating in a crowded restaurant. As sometimes happens in a crowd, there occurred a brief interlude when, for no apparent reason, everyone in the room stopped talking — everyone, that is, but young Donald.

"Daddy!" I cried, "tell us about the time you escaped from prison!"

Momentarily the room was in shock. Then suddenly everyone was laughing. (Why, I wondered, was Dad blushing so furiously?)

Trips to and from America must have been something of an ordeal for our poor parents. We were three brothers. Dick, the youngest, wasn't old enough to engage in much fraternal rivalry, but Bob and I were close to the same age, and when we weren't cooperating in some misadventure (like the time we upset a traveling prince and his retinue by scrambling their shoes, left overnight in the corridor to be shined), we often wrestled each other to work off excess energy.

Bob was born a year and a half after me, but soon grew to my height, and occasionally surpassed it. He felt little hesitancy in challenging a seniority which I had no intention of relinquishing. Temperamental differences existed between us, too. Bob was impulsive, outgoing, fond of popularity, demonstrative of his feelings. I was in many ways quite the opposite: reserved, rather shy, pensive, forever questioning. Bob once picked up a caterpillar from a path with the loving cry, "There, there, you poor little worm! I'll put you over here so no one can step on you." He then ran off gaily, quite forgetting the incident. Had I helped the same caterpillar, I would have pondered the incident for days, wondering what it was that made certain creatures defenseless, and why this particular insect, out of millions, should have received help. Beside Bob I'm afraid I sometimes felt myself rather a lump. As a matter of fact that thought seemed sometimes to bother him, too. His spirit of rivalry was, I think, rooted partly in unconscious disapproval of me for not being more like others. But for all that we managed to be good friends. And always, where the rest of the world was concerned, we stood together in brotherly solidarity, never more so than when either of us was being threatened.

Fighting is, I suppose, an inextricable part of the process of growing up, particularly so for boys. I recall what might be considered my fair share of boyhood scraps, though I don't remember ever instigating one. (In this respect I was unlike my cousin Ed, who made full, aggressive use of nature's gift to him of a strong body. "Eddy," his mother once admonished him, "don't you know that when another boy hits you, you shouldn't hit back?" "Oh, but Mother," Ed remonstrated self-righteously, "I *never* hit back. I always hit first!")

Though I myself never "hit first," if ever it seemed important to me to demonstrate to others, or to myself, that I was no coward I was not one to turn the other cheek. Several fights, in fact, far from stirring me now to repentance, stand out in my memory as having helped me to learn worthwhile lessons.

It was because of a fight that I first learned something of the fickleness of human loyalties. I was seven or eight at the time. Alvin, a big boy who was visiting Teleajen with his parents, determined to impose his command on our group. Brawn, fortunately, was not important to our "group dynamics." I knew that the support I had from my friends was born of mutual affection, not of fear. But when Alvin challenged me, his victory seemed so much a foregone conclusion that most of the children, fearing later retribution, sided with him. Bob was the sole exception. I, furious with the rest of them for their fickleness, determined to teach them a good lesson by beating Alvin.

It was a long, somewhat bloody battle. Every shout for Alvin only goaded me to renewed efforts. Gradually his strength flagged. As it began to look as if I might win after all, first one of the children, then another, joined Bob in rooting for me. At last Alvin's courage crumbled altogether. By this time everyone was enthusiastically on my side.

Victory was bittersweet for me that day, however. I knew my friends had really wanted me to win all along. But I also understood a little bit what an unreliable thing is the support of one's fellow creatures.

Wise indeed is he who discovers that God's friendship *alone* can never fail him.

But disappointment is a good teacher; it helps us to take our first, faltering steps out of childhood toward maturity. For the world is frequently at odds with our desires. The sign of maturity is a willingness to adjust to realities broader than one's own. It is how we react to disappointment that determines whether our development will be a shrinking towards bitterness and cynicism, or an expansion towards acceptance and wisdom.

Chapter Three

Storm Clouds

IT WAS SUMMER, 1935. I was nine years old. Vacationing in the quaint mountain village of Buşteni, I was enjoying a happy season of games, picnics on grassy meadows, and carefree laughter.

One afternoon I went to my room to read a book. Sitting in a chair, I suddenly felt dizzy. I lay down on the bed, but even from this position the room seemed to be spinning. I cried weakly for help, but no one came. At last, summoning all my strength, I struggled to the door, leaning against the wall for support, and called again. This time I was heard.

A doctor was hastily summoned. A large, loud-voiced, overconfident lady, she was evidently determined to prove that I had appendicitis. (*Prod.* "Does it hurt here?" *Prod again.* "How about here?") Minutes of this diagnostic predetermination made me hurt all over. Finally, deciding, perhaps, that it would be no use operating on my entire abdomen, she gave up.

I came near dying in that little village. As it was, though I survived, the happy world I had known for the first nine years of my life died for me with this illness. Back home in Teleajen, all I remember "clearly" are long stretches of delirium: Dad reading to me from Mark Twain's *Huckleberry Finn*, and the drunken fits of Huck's father returning to me at night in a terrifying garb.

"I don't *want* to be a drunkard!" I cried, wrestling with my own delirium. "I don't *want* to be a drunkard."

At last I came to associate *any* unusual mental state with delirium. The very soul-expansion which, until this time, had visited me so often at night, now filled me with a nameless dread.

Because of this fear, I now began making a conscious effort to adjust to the norms of others. For the better part of a decade, insecurity and self-doubt left me anxious to prove to myself that I was not in some indefinable way abnormal.

Dr. Stroyei, a pediatrician in Bucharest, finally diagnosed my illness as colitis. He forbade me all dairy products, and put me on a bland diet of soft-cooked foods that almost robbed me of all interest in eating. When I'd recovered sufficiently, my parents decided to send me to the salubrious climate of Switzerland. Dr. Winthrop Haynes, my godfather, recommended a small Swiss-English boarding school where his own sons had studied for a time, in

Chesières, a mountain village in French Switzerland. The school was named, perhaps a trifle pretentiously, *L'Avenir* ("The Future").

My own future here, eighteen long months of it, was somewhat bleak. Only nine years old when I arrived, never before away from my family, and unfamiliar with French (the language commonly spoken at L'Avenir), I was homesick much of the time. Throughout my stay, moreover, I was afflicted with a series of fairly serious illnesses, stemming from the colitis.

L'Avenir was owned and run by a kindly couple, Mr. and Mrs. John Hampshire. Mr. Hampshire was English; his wife, whom we children knew affectionately as Tante Béa (Aunt Beatrice), was French-Swiss. The students themselves were a mixed bag of Swiss, English, American (me), Italian, and French.

Unhappy though I was, my stay there did have its compensations. The scenery, for one thing, was stunningly beautiful. Across the valley from us loomed the famous Alp, Les Dents du Midi. In winter we skied daily. In warmer weather, frequent walks led us through flowered pastures and quiet, discreet woods — all very properly Swiss. I still recall the herds of cows passing our chalet school in the early mornings, their bells ringing melodiously.

Gradually, too, as I learned to speak French, adjustment became easier for me. The teachers, able to communicate with me now, grew quite fond of me. (Grownups were touched, generally, because I treated them like *people*.) Even our frosty German teacher, to whom I'd seemed merely stupid as long as I couldn't speak French, eventually thawed.

Storm Clouds

My long illness coincided with the growing political malady of Europe. In Vienna, where Mother and I stopped on our way to Switzerland, we were warned by friends not to criticize Nazi Germany except in safe places, and then only in whispers. Austria had not yet been annexed, but one saw Nazi officers everywhere, marching about, challenging people with the Nazi salute, sternly shouting, *"Heil Hitler!"* ("Hi," I would reply, waving a hand nonchalantly.) Storm clouds were gathering. In the bluster of bullies everywhere one saw the arrogance of men newly justified in their own eyes. And, growing in the hearts of peace-loving people everywhere, there was fear.

One of the students at L'Avenir was an Italian boy, larger by a head than most of us, and a braggart. Guido tried to ingratiate himself with us by laughing loudly at everything, and at nothing. But he was a bully, and nobody liked him. He was also — naturally enough, considering his own insensitivity — an ardent supporter of Italy's dictator, Mussolini. We were never allowed to forget his country's "glorious" conquest of poor, backward Abyssinia.

Little cogs in a big wheel! But it took those little cogs to make the wheel turn. Individual bullies, each insignificant in himself, were banding together on the stage of history, and imagined in their swelling ranks that fate had given them the power to change the world. For them it was a heady hour. Such, indeed, is the power of mass hysteria that ere long many others, too, peace-loving formerly, were striding about behaving like petty dictators.

An Austrian friend of ours in Teleajen, pleasant enough when he first came there, caught the bully fever. From then on, normal conversation with him was impossible; all he ever spouted was a succession of grim boasts. "We Germans," it seemed, would soon be marching in to subjugate everyone and his dog.

This man's chief weakness was simply, I think, that he lacked a sense of humor. I've never known a bully to possess one. I don't mean they can't laugh *at* people; that they do readily enough. It's that they can't laugh *with* others. Humor certainly was conspicuous by its absence among those who succumbed to the disease of Naziism.

I even wonder whether the evolution of tyranny isn't reducible to some kind of law, in which humorlessness plays an essential role. First, it seems, in the line of converts to tyranny come the true bullies — the sadists, the mentally crippled and vengeful, the criminal. Then, as the spirit of arrogance spreads, well-meaning but essentially humorless people enter to swell the tide. Finally come the well-meaning, but stupid. At this point, anyone with any true values has little choice but to flee, to go underground, or to maintain a resolute silence in the face of general insanity. Or — he can laugh.

One evening in Germany a famous comedian appeared on stage before a large audience. Clicking his heels together, he raised his right arm high above his head. Several people in the audience leapt to their feet and returned the Nazi salute.

"That," said the comedian, "is how high my dog jumped yesterday."

This man knew the probable consequences of his brave gesture, but his sense of humor in the face of those probabilities revealed that indomitable spirit in human nature before which tyranny must ever succumb in the end.

In the summer of 1936 we traveled through Germany on our way to America. A stranger sharing Bob's train compartment was arrested at the German border by the Gestapo. Perhaps he was Jewish. Or perhaps, like thousands of others, he was merely trying to flee despotism. But, young as we were at the time, we knew the likely outcome of his arrest: imprisonment, and then death.

In Rumania I had a governess for a time who, like our friend in Teleajen, was an Austrian Nazi. Also like him, she was quite devoid of any sense of humor. Miss Annie assured us constantly, whenever our parents weren't there to hear her, that Japan would never lose in any war against America, having never lost one in its long history. The German people, moreover, in league with the Japanese and the Italians, were destined to rule the whole world. It seemed peculiarly fitting to us when Miss Annie was found to be a kleptomaniac.

Whenever we traveled through Germany, however, all the people we met proved exceedingly kind and hospitable, eager to help us in every way they could. Were *these* people Nazis? Some, I suppose, were; the worst bully, after all, is still a child of God, and cannot but reflect something of the Divine Goodness. But I think most of them were simply normal, good people caught up in the flood of a national tragedy. We loved them almost more, I think, for the sadness of their plight. What country, after all, is in a position to be able to say honestly, "*Our* people would never sink so low"?

The plight of Europe affected me deeply. Why, I wondered, can't people learn to live together in harmony? What is it in human nature that courts, that seems almost to *demand*, tragedy?

Perhaps my gloomy reflections were aggravated by my own unhappiness. One day I was standing alone on the balcony of our chalet school. Mr. Hampshire came out to find me weeping silently.

"What's the matter?" he inquired gently.

"I'm homesick!" I sobbed.

Kindly, he wrote that day to my parents. Soon it was decided that I should return home.

During my stay in Switzerland Dad had been transferred to Bucharest. Our new residence was on the outskirts of the city, at Strada Capitan Dimitriade No. 10. Here I got six months' respite before resuming my formal education. It was during this period that Miss Annie tutored me.

My health through this winter of 1936-37 was still precarious. Occasionally the pain was intense, though I remember now, more clearly than the pain, the tears in Mother's eyes as she suffered with me in her love.

Sometimes, when I was well enough, I played football on an empty lot with the neighborhood children. One of these was a boy from a slum area across Boulevard Buşteni. His family were so poor they couldn't even afford window panes, but covered up the window openings in winter with newspapers. I took intense pity on him, invited him frequently to my home, and gave him freely of my toys. I was his friend. He, I assumed, was my friend.

One day he and a few of the boys in our own neighborhood taught me a hard lesson. Dissembling camaraderie, they invited me to join them in the courtyard of a nearby home. The gate closed quietly behind me; someone locked it. Then, to my surprise, they backed me against a fence and began kicking a football at me, trying to hit me with it. Obviously, they were working up the courage for an attack.

I stood my ground and waited quietly, struck the football aside whenever it came too near, and affected an attitude of indifference. Minutes passed. At last the boys changed their minds about the merits of this afternoon's entertainment. The gate was opened, and I was allowed to walk out unscathed.

Though physically unhurt, I thought my heart would break. Back home, I wept inconsolably. Why, I asked Mother through tears, had my "dearest" friend, and my other good companions, so betrayed my love for them? It was small comfort to reflect that war hysteria had by now made Rumanians suspicious of *all* foreigners.

Painful though this experience was, it proved an excellent lesson. From it I learned that it isn't enough to give to others, even with love. If one would not beggar them in their own eyes, one must make it in some way possible for them also to reciprocate.

My absence in Switzerland, which had relieved Bob of the restraining presence of an older brother, had left him by no means languishing in his new freedom. Gleefully in fact, from then on, he insisted

The Search

---

that every important event in our family must have occurred "while you were in Switzerland."

My absence from home had had its effect on me, too. Whether I liked it or not, I now was a little less dependent on the home for which I had so recently been feeling homesick. God was weaning me from dependence on earthly security. My illness; my consequent absence, in that condition, in a far land; my growing sense of aloneness: These were, I think, meant only to help me realize that my true home is not here, on earth, but in Him.

Indeed, this is for all men an eternal truth: God is our reality. Ineluctably we are led, quickly or slowly, by one path or another, towards this divine understanding.

In this thought I am reminded of a brother disciple who once asked our guru, "Will I ever leave the spiritual path?"

"How could you?" the master answered. "Everyone in the world is on the spiritual path."

My parents in Teleajen, Rumania, a few days after my appearance on the scene, May, 1926

My mother and I
(my first Christmas)

My brothers Dick and Bob, and I (top left). If Dick was one year old at the time, I was five

Ella Todd Quarles, my maternal grandmother

My mother as a child

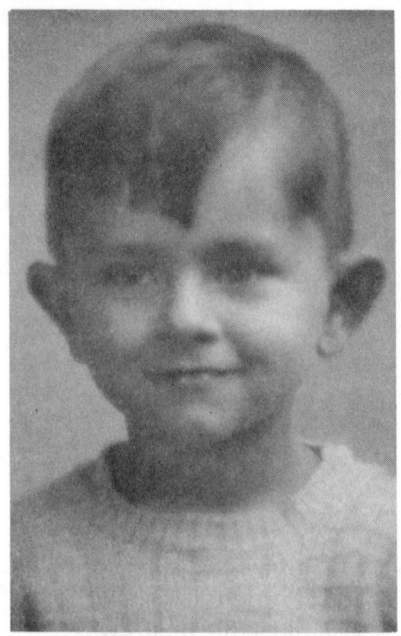
At age four in Teleajen

My mother, Gertrude
G. Walters

My father, Ray
P. Walters

In school in Switzerland

Bucharest, age ten

Chapter Four

A Temporary Haven

PERHAPS THE DIVINE FISHERMAN was thinking this poor fish had better not be pulled in too forcibly, lest he break the line. At any rate, the process of dragging me out of my little pond of earthly security became, for a time, relatively pleasant for me. After six months in Bucharest my health was greatly improved. I was eleven years old now, and my parents were anxious to see me resume my formal education.

A Quaker boys' school in England had been highly recommended to us. Nestling snugly in the heart of the Malvern Hills near the village of Colwall, The Downs School was surrounded by verdant, rolling fields, and by narrow country roads that wound their way carefully between clipped, very *English* hedges. The buildings were attractive, and the grounds spacious. I was steeled to the idea, which months earlier had been so painful to me, of living away from home. The Downs seemed a better place than most in which to spend my exile.

The English have many wonderful traits: honor, loyalty, a sense of duty and fair play. Since, however, this is a chronicle of my spiritual search, I cannot in good conscience ignore what comes across to me as a certain blind spot in their national temperament: a reliance so complete on the ordinary that it gives almost no credence to the extraordinary. Something there is about the religious spirit of England that tries to mold Jesus Christ himself into the very proper image of an English gentleman, and casts the Old Testament prophets as fellow club members with him, perhaps writing occasional letters to the *Times* in protest against the lamentable want of good form in a few of their countrymen. Whether members of the Church of England or of any other sect, the English give one the impression of having neatly clipped and trimmed their religion, like a hedge, to protect values that are primarily social. I refer not to the courageous free-thinking few, but to the many whose worship seems to close, rather than open, windows onto infinity.

I hope I am wrong. At any rate, the only memorable religious event for me during my two years at The Downs occurred one Sunday evening when the father of one of our students, an Anglican minister, delivered a sermon. This man's body, almost perfectly round, was surmounted by a face that was dangerously suggestive of a pig's — dangerously, I say, because his porcine appearance, combined with a spirit of immense dignity, reduced me and a friend beside me to helpless fits of merriment. All I remember clearly now is looking up at one point, through tears, to see "the pig" describing a wide circle with his arms. "And the whole world ..." he cried feelingly. His gesture so perfectly outlined his own global figure that fresh paroxysms of mirth overwhelmed us. The row directly behind ours was filled with faculty members, but to my surprise none of them endeavored to discipline us. Perhaps they, too, were finding self-control difficult!

The Downs was easily the best school I ever attended. Religious teaching there may not have been exactly ponderous, but in other respects the teachers knew how to draw the best out of their students. Character building is more basic to the English educational system than to the American. At The Downs, honor, fair play, truthfulness, and a sense of responsibility were given strong emphasis. To tell a lie was considered almost beneath contempt. A boy was once caught stealing sixpence and a little candy from another boy's locker, and so shocked everyone that he was expelled from the school.

In sports, too, though we did our best to win, we were taught that the game itself, not its outcome, was what really mattered. After rugby matches with other schools the members of both teams dined together, rivalry forgotten, new friendships affirmed. I have sometimes wondered what would happen if opposing teams in America were to dine together following a game. Given our national emphasis on winning, I suspect there might be a free-for-all.

Once, in punishment for some pecadillo, a group of us were told to run several miles around a course of country roads. No one checked up on us to make sure we didn't spend that time lying under some tree instead. Mr. Hoyland, the headmaster, knew it wouldn't occur to us to break our word to him.

Another time, as punishment for some infraction, I was told not to go swimming on three occasions when I really wanted to. The trust implied in this condition helped me to live up to it, though I must admit that on one of those occasions it was raining, so I wouldn't have been able to go anyway.

Needless to say, idealism didn't always win out over basic human weaknesses, nor propriety over boyhood's natural exuberance. But on the whole I am impressed with what the English school system was able to accomplish.

The Downs School had a number of innovative features of its own: two kinds of marks, for example, one of them in Greek letters, to show how well we'd done in the subjects themselves; and the other in colors, to show how earnestly we'd applied ourselves to those subjects. Those bright colors seemed somehow even more worth striving for than the letter grades.

Wednesday afternoons were our hobby time. We were allowed to select our own hobbies, on approval, and were given qualified instructors for them. My first year there I studied sculpture; my second, painting. For what would have been my third year, a group of us generated enough interest to get astronomy approved. But for me, as will become clear later on, that year was not destined to be.

In addition to sculpture and painting I studied piano, and also sang in the choir. Our choir instructor, a puffy-cheeked, solemn, but good-natured lady, would peer at us myopically as she waved her baton. With great earnestness she taught us to sing:

> Bach and Handel, as you know
> Died and were buried long ago.
> Born in the year one-six-eight-five,
> Still they're very much alive.

If this ditty fell short of the musical standards it celebrated, we had no quarrel with the sentiment it expressed. For we loved classical music. Actually I seldom heard popular music until we moved to America. My parents and their friends occasionally threw parties and danced to records, but to us boys this was just "grown-up nonsense." I remember how we shook with merriment the time I imitated for my brothers a recording I'd heard in England of "My Dear Mister Shane," sung in extravagantly nasal accents by the Andrews Sisters. At the Downs, too, tastes ran generally to classical music, except perhaps among the older boys. It was quite unselfconscious on our part; we simply liked it.

Too many people treat the classics as though they were something to be bolted down with water and a wry face. But if children's tastes weren't conditioned otherwise by their sexually awakened elders, I think most of them might grow up loving great music.

Life in England exposed me also to another kind

of sound: the British accent. Not that I was unfamiliar with it; many of our friends in Rumania were English. But there at least we mixed with them on neutral ground. Here only I was a foreigner. Placed at such a disadvantage, I worked hard to overcome it. By the time I returned home for my first vacation I was already saying "ne-oh," and "shahn't" with the best of 'em — much to the dismay of my parents.

At first I tried awkwardly to cloak my shyness under a somewhat ill-fitting mantle of jocularity. A boy named Randall decided my behavior lacked proper dignity for a Downs boy. When I passed off his scolding with another joke, he became so irritated that he challenged me to a fight. Randall was the accepted leader of our form,* and was accustomed to being obeyed.

Grudges at The Downs weren't supposed to be settled on the spot. To win time for a possible reconciliation, the rule was to submit a formal challenge, after which a boxing match was arranged in the gym, complete with seconds and a referee.

I accepted Randall's challenge. The date for the match was set. As the days passed, and Randall observed in me no sign of fear, his attitude toward me gradually changed.

"Let's be friends," he suggested one day. I assured him I'd never felt we were enemies. In time our friendship developed into one of the happiest I have ever known.

Randall was good-natured, highly intelligent, sensitive yet practical, and intensely earnest in everything he did. His friendship opened for me the

*The English equivalent of *grade*.

door to acceptance by the other boys. Once accepted, I brought to them a lighter spirit — the ability, for example, to laugh at oneself. Our Latin teacher, Mr. Days, a formidable man whose bluff I somehow managed to penetrate, wrote to me years later, "Yours wasn't, perhaps, the brightest class I ever had, but it was certainly the happiest."

Days passed in study, good fellowship, and sports. A fast runner, I managed to play wing three-quarter (the principal running position) in several of the rugby games with other schools. Cricket, however, I considered an utter waste of a sunny afternoon. In practice sessions, which were obligatory, I would lie down in the outfield and wait comfortably for someone to shout, "Walters, get up! The ball's coming your way!"

Sometimes there were inter-form "wars" — in fun, not in anger. One form would "board" the other, perhaps through windows that hadn't been secured quickly enough. Fights at The Downs, even those initiated in anger, commonly strengthened the spirit of friendship. This was an outcome that, to my surprise, I never encountered in the schools I attended later in America.

But while we scrapped and competed merrily in classrooms and on the playing fields, another more serious conflict was developing in Europe. The relentless appoach of World War II made a somber backdrop to our schooldays, one that was never very far from our thoughts. Many of us, we realized, might have to fight in the next war. Many of us would probably be killed.

The pride of the English is intense. One boy, dignifying with the label of patriotism what was really only a mean nature, once called me a "dirty foreigner." I was inured to the second half of this role, so didn't feel greatly offended. "If I'm a dirty foreigner," I replied, smiling, "perhaps you're a dirty Englishman." Outraged, the boy leapt at me. I proved stronger than he, and had no difficulty in holding him down till he tired of hurling imprecations and cooled off. Later I related the incident to Randall and one or two other friends, and was impressed at the depth of their patriotic feeling. Their laughter at the outset was generous; none of them liked the boy, and all of them liked me. But it subsided when I reached the point where I'd said, "Perhaps you're a dirty Englishman." Their sympathy returned only when I explained that it was purely a question of whether or not the other boy had recently bathed.

England's Prime Minister, Sir Neville Chamberlain, went to Germany in 1938, and returned with the welcome proclamation, "Peace in our time." Much was made in the press of his glad tidings, though I don't think people put much faith in them. At any rate, gas masks were soon passed out to each of us at school. On a trip to Rumania with Roy Redgrave, the son of family friends of ours there, we sang the English national anthem loudly in the streets of Nuremberg, feeling very brave, though I don't suppose the Gestapo felt particularly threatened by a couple of skinny English schoolboys. What children do, however, reflects the spirit of their elders. Throughout Europe, defiance was now in the air. It could only be a matter of time before open conflict broke out.

My two years in England gave me much to be grateful for. The friendships I formed there, and the good times we had, left me with many happy memories. Though circumstances prevented me from returning for my third and final year, Mr. Hoyland had selected me for the second half of that year to be the head boy. But my gain was not only in the form of memories. I also learned many worthwhile lessons, particularly on the correctness or incorrectness of different patterns of behavior. Such teaching borders on an important spiritual principle. For as my guru was to emphasize later, it is not enough to be guided by high ideals: One must also "learn to behave." That is to say, one must know how to relate properly to every reality on its own level.

This balance of the inner and outer aspects of one's life is not easy to achieve. My two years in England helped me toward this fulfillment. Partly for this reason, England has always held a warm place in my heart. So great is my regard for the fine characteristics of her people, and so loving were the friendships I formed there, that I think I shall always remain, in part, an Englishman.

Chapter Five

The Storm Breaks

IT WAS SPRING, 1939. Dad, after fifteen years in Rumania, had risen to become head geologist for Esso in Europe. Now he was being transferred to Zagreb, Yugoslavia, there to be Esso's exploration manager. All our belongings were packed and stored in Bucharest, ready for shipment. In March Dad rented an apartment in The Hague, Holland, on Königinegracht. We spent our Easter vacation there. (Fond memories of picturesque streets, acres of tulips, and smiling, friendly people!)

Summer came, and with it another visit to America. The weeks passed quietly for us among relatives in Ohio and Oklahoma. August was about to close its ledger; it was time for us to return to Europe. We entrained at Tulsa for New York.

The Storm Breaks

As we stepped out onto the station platform in Chicago, the headline struck us with all the force of an ocean wave: *WAR!* Hitler had invaded Poland. Hopes for peace had been smashed on rocks of hatred and nationalistic greed. To return now to a war-torn continent would be foolish. Dad was transferred to the head offices of Esso at Rockefeller Center, in New York City. Our belongings, packed and ready for shipment to Zagreb, had only to be rerouted to America.

We settled eventually in the New York suburb of Scarsdale, at 90 Brite Avenue, in the Foxmeadow section. For the next nine years this was to be my home, or rather my point of perennial departure.

While I was still a small child my parents had enrolled me at Kent School, in Kent, Connecticut. This was a church school for boys, run by Episcopalian monks. I was not scheduled to enter Kent for another year, however, and was placed meanwhile at Hackley, a boys' school near Tarrytown, New York.

And now the Divine Fisherman began once again to reel in His line determinedly. Looking back after all these years, it is easier for me to summon up a certain proper sense of gratitude to God for holding me so closely in check. At that time, however, I'm afraid gratitude was not my uppermost sentiment. A month earlier my expectations had been glowing. I was returning to The Downs for a happy final year there, surrounded by good friends. Now suddenly I found myself, at thirteen, the youngest boy in the lowest grade of a high school where the only familiar feature was my own perennial status as a "foreigner," a status which, as a born American returning to his own country to live, I found particularly distasteful.

Even my accent, now English, set me apart. But whereas formerly, in England, my American accent had occasioned little more than good-natured amusement, here my English accent marked me for derision. It took me at least a year to learn to "talk American" once again.

Heretofore in my life I had never heard a dirty word. At Hackley it seemed, once I'd been initiated into the new vocabulary, that I heard little else. In the past, swing music had been only an amusing game. Here, it was practically a religion. Sex had never before figured in our conversations. Here, it was virtually an obsession. Aggressive behavior, rudeness, insensitivity to others as an affirmation of one's own independence — these, it seemed, were the norms. School "wisdom" included such precious advice as, "Silence is golden — and also healthy."

The fact that I was just entering puberty made the problem of adjustment all the more difficult. In truth, I could see no good reason to adjust. Rather, I tended to enclose myself defensively within psychic walls, like a medieval town under attack. One or two of the boys were friendly to me, but to the others I seemed merely an import, dumped on American soil quite unnecessarily, and, considering the solid worth of the domestic article, even presumptuously.

In the room next to mine there was a boy of fifteen, named Tommy, who weighed two hundred and twenty pounds to my one hundred and seven.

The Storm Breaks

Tommy was a bully. My "English ways" were, to him, an insult to the glory of America. It wasn't long before, dissatisfied with merely voicing his disapproval, he advanced to open threats.

I'm not sure he was quite sane. One morning I awoke to see him peering in my window, an air pistol in his hand. As I leapt to safety behind my desk, a bullet struck the other side of it with a thud.

What bothered Tommy about me, I think, was not only the implied insult of my un-American ways, but the fact that I wouldn't acknowledge my self-evident inferiority by cringing before him. Later that day he made it a point to sit next to me at lunch, the better to express his opinions. Throughout the meal he criticized my appearance, my vocabulary, my table manners. ("Don't you know you should spoon your soup toward the *far* side of the bowl — peasant?") I paid no attention to him. Finally he muttered, "Boy, am I going to get you!"

I knew he meant it. Back in my room after lunch I pushed the dresser up against the door, which was without a lock. Tommy arrived shortly afterward, breathing threats. He rattled the doorknob, then leaned heavily against the door, puffing dire predictions with mounting fury. At last, succeeding in shoving the door open, he rushed into the room like an enraged bull and proceeded to beat me with such uncontrolled rage that it really seemed as if he wanted to kill me.

"I'm going to throw you out that window!" he panted again and again. (We were three stories above the ground.) Throughout the beating he kept his voice low for fear of attracting the attention of others on our floor. Somehow the ferocity of his whisper sounded more invidious than an angry shout.

What could I do, small as I was? I lay motionless on the bed, face down, waiting for him to exhaust himself.

"Why didn't you cry for help?" a friend asked me the next day.

"Because I wasn't afraid."

Interestingly, the fact that I took Tommy's beating calmly, and never thereafter altered my attitude toward him, left him without another weapon to use against me.

People commonly see physical victory as conclusive. But true victory is always mental. One's conqueror may feel conquered in turn by a spirit that he finds he cannot reach with physical weapons.

Tommy, from this time on, gave me a wide berth.

Though released now from his bullying, in other respects my life at Hackley grew no happier. I sought escape in the music room, where for hours at a time I practice the piano. My unhappiness stirred me also for the first time to a longing for the religious life. Perhaps, I thought, I would become a missionary. I expressed these aspirations, somewhat hesitantly, to my cousin Betty, when both of us were at my parents' home in Scarsdale. She was horrified.

"Not a missionary, Don! There's too much to *do* in this world. You wouldn't want to bury yourself on some primitive island!"

The vigor of her reaction shook me in my still-frail resolution. What, after all, did I really know about the missionary calling? Self-doubt was in any case becoming my own private hell.

After a year at Hackley School, the time came for me to enter Kent.

Kent is an Ivy League prep school that ranks high, scholastically and socially. I entered it with high hopes. But I soon found that the general interests of the boys here were essentially what they had been at Hackley, with the addition of a sort of "All for God, Country, and Our School Team" spirit in which arrogance played the leading part. The Kent student was expected by his peers to embrace every social norm, to like or dislike all the "right" people, and to boast of his proficiency in all the "right" activities, particularly those related to sex and drinking. Woe betide that hapless youth who danced to a different piper. To laugh with the loudest, to tell the dirtiest jokes, to shout boisterously when merely passing the time of day, to smile expansively at everyone ("Oh, *hi*, Don!") in a bid to get *others* to like *you:* These were the banners of success. Conformity made one eligible for that supreme reward: popularity. Nonconformity exiled one to a limbo of disapproval and contempt.

Experience had shown me that I had the ability to make friends. But what was I to do when, try as I might, I simply couldn't share the enthusiasms of my fellow students? It was not a question, as it had been in England, of relating to new realities on their own level. In England, principles at least had been concerned. Here I could find none — only egotism, selfishness, and self-interest. I might have been able to stand my ground firmly had I been able to outshout, out-boast, and out-laugh others. As it was, being naturally somewhat shy, I was unwilling to offer my ideas where I felt they were unwelcome.

Instead I became intensely introverted, miserable with myself, certain that my life was already, at its outset, a failure. In an environment that demanded absolute conformity, an inability to conform seemed like failure indeed. Gradually it became as evident to others as it already was to me that I was simply one of that unfortunate breed, of which the human race will ever produce its allotted few: a misfit, a general embarrassment, a creature of subnormal ability.

Yet in my heart I knew this judgment to be false.

I tried my best to enter into the life of the school. I joined the school paper, reporting sports events with a hopeful heart. But my first two articles spelled my undoing; my humorous touch on so sacred a subject as *sports* was considered tantamount to blasphemy. The editor smiled with amusement, then appeased his conscience by withholding further assignments from me. I joined the debating society, but found I couldn't speak in defense of issues to which I wasn't sincerely committed. I became a member of the French club, but my fellow members were for the most part lonely outcasts like me. I played football. I rowed. I sang in the glee club.

Nothing worked. There was almost a kind of shame in the few friendships I did form, a tacit understanding that ours was a companionship in failure.

At times I was actually afraid to leave a roomful

of boys, lest my departure give them the opportunity to talk against me. Nor were my fears groundless: I knew, from the times when I stayed, what uncomplimentary things they could say about those less popular boys who happened to be absent. One day, after passing a couple of classmates on the stairway in our dormitory, I overheard one of them, obviously not caring whether I heard him or not, laugh derisively, "What a sad case!"

The worst of it was, I had no clear grounds on which to refute him.

During this gloomy period, religion might have been the comfort for me that it had been at Hackley. Kent was, after all, a church school, and most of the boys there were moderately religious; at least, I recall none of them grumbling over the required attendance at worship services. But religion at Kent seemed as though it were being kept preserved in formaldehyde. With the exception of one jolly, elderly brother who taught no classes, and who was, I'm afraid, a little foolish, the monks seemed a joyless lot, uninspired and uninspiring in their calling. The church services were heavy with the consciousness that one went through all this merely because it was *done*. Religion at Kent inspired me to look almost anywhere but to God for solace and enlightenment.

Soon I was seeking both of these fulfillments in the realm of ideas. Always a bookworm, I began diving into the worlds of James Fenimore Cooper, Sir Walter Scott, Keats, Shelley, Shaw, and other great writers.

At fourteen I began writing a novel of my own.

The Search

The influence of Cooper was evident in my setting: A pioneer family, living on an isolated farm in Oklahoma, was attacked by red Indians. Only two boys escaped massacre, by fleeing during the confusion. Earnestly, at this point, I counseled the reader not to think harshly of the Indians, "For they had been oppressed by the white man ever since he came to this continent, and had had their hunting grounds taken away and changed into towns and places of civilization ... Nor must you think ill of their scalping methods, for that was just the coustom [sic] among the Indians, and though we may think it cruel or repulsive, surely some of the things we do are just as bad, if not more so."

The two boys escaped into a nearby forest, pursued by Indians. Deep in the forest they discovered a cliff, scaled it to a high ledge, and there rested, thinking they'd arrived unobserved. Minutes later, one of them happened to look down from their ledge, "and drew back in astonishment, for there, not five feet below him, was an Indian, and following him came three more, the last two carrying guns, but the others without them for greater agility. Just then the foremost one heard him and uttered a word that would correspond to our word 'Shucks!' For they had planned on a surprise." (How I've laughed over that Indian's disappointed exclamation!)

The boys, having nowhere else to go, fled into a nearby cave. Down and down it led them, deep under the surface of the earth. At last, to their amazement, they emerged into another world, inexplicably sunlit and beautiful. Here Indians and white men lived happily together in perfect brotherhood: hence the title of the novel, *The Happy Hunting Grounds*.

This was all, of course, pure escapism. Yet it also reflected a feeling which I think comes to many people from time to time in their lives: the deep inner certainty that their true home *is* elsewhere, that they belong in heaven, and that the present world is only a proving ground for the soul. As Jesus said, "No man hath ascended up to heaven, but he that came down from heaven."* This certainty is born not of speculation, but of deep astral memories that have been dimmed by more recent, earthly experiences.

Unhappiness and suffering are necessary for the soul's unfoldment. Without them we might remain satisfied with petty fulfillments. Worse still, we might remain satisfied with *ourselves*.** My personal unhappiness at Kent School inspired me to meditate on the sufferings of mankind everywhere. Could anything, I wondered, be done to improve the human lot?

Surely, if all men would truly accept one another as equals they would be much happier. I laboriously worked out a system of government in which no man possessed any personal property, all things being owned in common. Though I don't think I realized it at the time, my ideas were similar in several respects to those preached, though hardly prac-

---

*John 3:13
**"Because thou sayest, I am rich, and increased with goods, and have need of nothing; and knowest not that thou art wretched, and miserable, and poor, and blind, and naked: I counsel thee to buy of me gold tried in the fire ... and anoint thine eyes with eyesalve, that thou mayest see." (Revelation 3:17,18.)

ticed, under modern communism. But as I pondered the matter more deeply, I came to realize that most men are not capable of living in a voluntary state of nonpossession. A few people — monks, for instance — might be nonattached enough to consider nothing their own, but to *force* nonpossession on humanity at large would be tyranny. Dictatorship, even in the name of the common weal, would inflict more abuses than it could alleviate.

At this time also I wrote a one-act play, titled, *The Peace Treaty*. Its subtitle was, "Every Man for Himself." It was about a group of cave men, tribal chieftains, who got together after a war to determine the conditions for peace. One of them, like all visionaries ahead of his times, proposed an idea that he claimed would banish war forevermore. His plan demanded a generous spirit of international cooperation among the different tribes to replace the inter-tribal rivalries and selfishness that had prevailed hitherto. The other chieftains professed great admiration for his ideas. But it soon became clear that they understood him not at all, for when it came to the question of what sacrifices each would have to make to ensure peace, each suggested a few "minimal" improvements in the original plan, with a view to getting as many concessions as possible for himself. The peace treaty was finally thrown out as chieftains scrambled for whatever booty each could grab for himself.

At the close of the play the hero soliloquized: "If God existed, would He allow all this? ... But — of course He exists! How could life have come to this earth without Him? Ah! I see it all now. Yes, God exists, but He wishes mankind to live under hard conditions, for it is only under such that Man can prove himself worthy of the Kingdom of Heaven." God cares, I concluded, but wants man to *earn* His blessings, for without victory over greed, paradise itself would become but another battleground. Man, I was saying, is not perfectible through outward systems, but only in himself. The play ended with blows and shouts offstage, followed by gunshots, then cannonades, then bombs, and finally one bomb, mightier than all the rest. And after that: *silence*.

The hard reality of human greed was the stumbling block on which my dreams of political salvation became shattered. At fifteen I began writing another novel, about a man who foresaw the destruction of modern civilization, and decided to do what he could to preserve its most constructive elements. Far out into the wilderness he went, and there built a utopian community. Aiding him were experts in various fields, men and women who understood that expertise must be rooted in wisdom and love, not merely in knowledge. This little community kept the lamp of civilization burning while the rest of humanity bombed itself back to the caves. The group then returned to their fellow men to teach them a better, more constructive way of life.

The more I thought about my visionary community, the more compellingly it attracted me. From an escapist dream my concept evolved gradually to a spreading network of intentional villages *within* the framework of present-day civilization. Someday, I resolved, I would start such a community myself.

It isn't often that one's boyhood dreams are later fulfilled. With God's grace, this one has been. That tale, however, must await its telling until a later chapter.

I gave much thought also at Kent to the possibility of paranormal phenomena — prophecy, telepathy, and the mental control of objective events — and to the question of what life is like after death. I wondered whether I might serve my fellow man better if I tried to develop extra-sensory powers myself. But no, I decided, this whole subject was too remote from common experience to be meaningful to most people. Instead I would become a writer; through words perhaps I would be able to inspire others to a loftier vision.

While I was mentally improving the world, however, my own little world was deteriorating rapidly. A few of the older boys conceived what must have been almost a hatred of me. Ineptness I suppose they might have excused; not everyone, after all, could hope to match them in their excellence. But while self-admittedly inept in their ways, I had gone on from this recognition of failure to develop other — to them, inadmissible — interests. Was not this implied rejection of their standards unthinkably presumptuous? They began openly threatening to make my life "really miserable" next year, when a few of them would be returning to Kent as student body leaders.

I felt I could take no more. In tears that summer I pleaded with Mother to take me home.

Stroking my head tenderly, she said, "I know,

dear. I know. You're like your Dad. He's always been shy when people didn't want what he had to give them. Yet he has so much to offer. And so do you. People haven't understood it, but never mind. Stay home now, and live with us who love you. Here you'll be happy."

What relief flooded my heart! I never saw Kent again. Who can say whether I might yet have coaxed a few useful lessons from its dreary walls? But I felt I had taken from them every blessing that I possibly could. I was ready now, inwardly as well as outwardly, for a different kind of schooling.

Teenage portrait

In front of our Scarsdale home

Chapter Six

A Paper Rest House: the "Popularity Game"

MOST OF THE YOUNG PEOPLE I met during my adolescence seemed secure in their values. The Nineteen-Forties were unlike today, when it is common for young people to question society's values, to seek Meaning, to ponder their relationship to the universe and to God. When I was in high school, as nearly as I could tell I walked alone in such questing. I knew no guidelines to follow. I wasn't even sure what it was I was seeking. All I knew definitely was that I wanted *something*, and that that something didn't seem to be what anyone else wanted.

Others had already planned their lives more or less confidently. They would get good jobs, make money, get ahead in the world, marry, settle down in Scarsdale or in some other wealthy community, raise children, throw cocktail parties, and enjoy the fruits of a normal, worldly life. But I already knew I didn't want money. I didn't want to "get ahead" materially. I wasn't interested in marrying and raising a family. I knew well enough a few of the things I *didn't* want, but had no distinct notion of what it was I *did* want. And in this uncertainty I sometimes doubted whether my disinclination for the things others prized wasn't proof of some inadequacy in myself.

Had others, I wondered, secure as they evidently were in their norms, achieved some insight to which I was blind? Certainly my lifelong inability to adopt a conventional outlook had for years been a source of intense unhappiness to me.

Now that I had left Kent, and was enrolled as a senior in Scarsdale High School, I determined to overcome what was surely a defect in my character. This new school year, I decided, I would try a great experiment. I would pretend to myself that I *liked* what everyone else liked, that their values were my values, their norms mine. I would see whether, by deliberately adopting their outlook, I could not begin at last to feel at home with it. If I succeeded, how easy my life would become! Resolutely I set my sights. This last year of high school would mark my giant step forward into normality.

As a first step toward "swinging with the crowd," I seized energetically on swing music. Every week I listened eagerly to the radio with my brothers to learn which popular songs had made it onto the Hit Parade. I put on crowd-consciousness like a suit, and soon found that it fit snugly enough.

A Paper Rest House: the "Popularity Game"

In shouting competitions I pitched in and shouted. In laughing I bubbled with the best. I dated. I danced. I became the vocalist for a local dance band. And as I made a great noise I found, incredibly, that I both liked it and was liked for it.

I began the school year with a major advantage: Both of my brothers were popular. Bob, who was in the tenth grade, was loved by everyone, including upperclassmen. His was not the typical attitude of the Big Man on Campus — more interested, that is to say, in being loved than in loving, and ever careful to associate with only the "right" people. Bob genuinely liked *everyone*. It made no difference to him whether they were looked up to or down on by others. He was their friend, and they knew it. Unable to tone his voice lower than a gentle boom, he dominated every gathering, but no one seemed to mind. Somehow in his company they felt more generous, more sure of their own goodness.

His enthusiasm for life was boundless. One day, coming home from playing in a football game, he was found to have a fever of 105°. Ill as he was, he had insisted on finishing the game.

They called him "Bucky," after Bucky Walters, the famous baseball player. Though the nickname has remained with him, I myself have never used it, for I know that he has also a deeper side, one that he doesn't often reveal to others — a refined sensitivity to music, a deep gentleness, a certain nobility of character, all of which seem to me rather betrayed by the hail-fellow-well-met implications in that nickname.

From the start it was obvious to everyone that

The Search

Bob and I were very different specimens. A few of my classmates, besides, had heard from Phil Boote, my ex-roommate at Kent. Phil also lived in Scarsdale, and had shown enough sense of community responsibility to warn them what a social disaster I was. For Bob's sake, however, and because I was so obviously determined to mend my unconventional ways, they gave me the benefit of the doubt, and accepted me kindly enough into their midst.

Scarsdale High was much larger than Kent, a fact which permitted many different types there to mix happily without the same pressure being placed on them to conform as there had been at Kent. Being Bob's brother automatically threw me into the "in" group, a position I boldly accepted as the kind of challenge I needed to bring off my "great experiment" with a maximum of success.

I tried out for the football team. At 136 pounds, I was hardly first-string material. Still, I played hard during practice sessions, and at the games ardently supported our team from the bench. Unfortunately for my dreams of glory, I was a halfback, and so also was Charlie Rensenhouse, the team captain. Openings in that position were rare. The only time I actually made it onto the playing field during a game was once when Rensenhouse got hurt.

"Walters, get out there and help Rensenhouse off the field."

In track I did better. We hadn't had a track team at Kent, so I was unfamiliar with the proper starting techniques, but I was a fast runner, and managed to acquit myself creditably. I actually ran the 100-yard dash in only 10.2 seconds at my first meet. Unfortunately, I pulled a ligament early in the season and was out of the running for the rest of the school year.

Of my classes, my favorite was English. Lucyle Hook, our English teacher, took a keen interest in her subject, loved her students, and obviously wanted with all her heart to share her knowledge with us. She was as much our friend as our teacher. With her encouragement I wrote short stories and poems. While none of them was particularly consequential, they were good enough at least to gain me a reputation as a budding talent, and fanned my determination to become a writer.

One of the students in my French class was a girl named Ruth, later voted the most beautiful girl in our senior class. I dated her frequently, and became as infatuated with her as any boy is likely to be with his first girlfriend. But there were potholes on the highway of our romance.

Dad, for fear of spoiling us boys, gave us a weekly allowance of only fifty cents. I had to save for two weeks merely to take Ruth out to the movies. Even then, we usually had to walk the several miles to White Plains and back. It wasn't the best possible setup for making a good impression on a girl.

Worse still, when it came to something so deeply personal as romance I couldn't put on my extroverted bluff, which was carrying me along successfully enough in other departments of my life. Somehow I'd conceived the notion that I was physically unattractive, and that I had nothing worthwhile really to offer anyone. Because I doubted my own worth, moreover, I was afraid to trust myself to another person's feelings about me. When another boy, a large, perennially joking, popular football star, began dating Ruth, I hadn't the self-confidence to compete with him. For that matter, I wouldn't have competed with him even if I'd been bursting with confidence, for I could never see love in the light of self-imposition and conquest.

Singing I found a joy. Mr. Hubbard, our chorus director, tried to persuade me to take it up as a career. "There's money in your voice," he would insist, not realizing that money was probably the poorest lure he could have dangled before me. That year I sang in Handel's *Messiah*, and in Gilbert and Sullivan's *Yeomen of the Guard*. At Our Church of St. James the Less, my brothers and I also sang the roles of the three wise men in the Christmas pageant, an event which, I was surprised to learn recently, is still remembered by some old-timers in Scarsdale.

Other activities at the church, I must admit, held less appeal for me. Our minister, Father Price, kept threatening us in his sermons that if we didn't toe the straight and narrow we'd soon end up "right in the lap of the Nazis."

Instead, I began bending rather too far in another direction. Doug Burch, a friend of Bob's and mine, introduced me to Nick's, a night club in Greenwich Village, famous as a hangout for Dixieland jazz enthusiasts. Eddie Condon, Peewee Russell, and other jazz "greats" played here with such consummate skill that I actually found myself growing to like jazz. Fascinated with this new "scene," I absorbed all its trivia: how the wife of one of the taller players used to beat him up; how the band ate in a night club across the street because

Nick wouldn't feed them properly; how a little old lady showed up on Saturday nights, took a front table, and clapped her hands enthusiastically to the music, shouting, "Yeah! Yeah!" like any teenager. It is amazing that people can make as much as they do out of this kind of "news," merely because celebrities are involved. But they do. And we did.

It was at Nick's that I took my first alcoholic drink. Of all the foolish pastimes to which mankind is given, drinking must surely rank near the top of the list. Few people, I imagine, take up either drinking or smoking for pleasure alone. It seems more a question of not wanting to appear gauche. At any rate, those were my motives. Alcohol I found at least not positively sickening, but smoking was like learning to enjoy rotten food.

I remember clearly the first time I learned to inhale. A girl at a party in Scarsdale showed me the knack. One drag made me so dizzy I almost slipped to the floor. Then, with the kind of inverted idealism that marked most of that year for me, I told myself sternly, "I'm going to *master* this thing if it kills me!" Little did I realize that *true* mastery would have meant not succumbing to such silliness in the first place. That evening I succeeded in "mastering" smoking, but I'm afraid it wasn't long before smoking mastered me.

The worst of drinking, from a spiritual standpoint, is not the temporary stupor it may induce, nor the hangover that sometimes follows an indiscreet "night on the town," but the long-range effect that alcohol exerts on the personality. In some subtle way it seems to make one more worldly; one's perceptions become less refined; one inclines, if ever so slightly, to scoff at things that he formerly considered sacred. The ego, in becoming less sensitively responsive to its environment, becomes more self-assertive and aggressive. It is as if it were gripping harder in an effort to compensate for the diminution of its natural powers. These effects, as I say, may be observed not only during hours of inebriation, but as actual, long-term personality changes.

The explanation may be that things, inert though they seem, actually serve as media for various states of consciousness. We may scoff, as I used to do, at "holy Joes" in church who denounce "likker" as a tool of Satan, but many a truth has been hooted down with laughter. The very inclination, so common in societies where drinking is popular, to tell jokes about drunkenness suggests a subconscious desire to silence the whisper of conscience. For every man must know deep inside him that drunkenness is an insult to his true divine nature.

Another "thing" through which consciousness often gets changed is music. Looking back, I am astonished to see how quickly, by my constant, *willing* exposure to swing music, I came to assume attitudes that I had thought formerly quite foreign to me. As months passed it became more and more my second nature to see life in terms of sports, romance, and good times, to laugh with the loudest, roam hither and yon with the most restless, and give and take in the youthful exuberance of an ego competing more or less insensitively with other egos.

Yet somewhere, deep inside me, there was a watchful friend who remained unimpressed, who questioned my motives, observed my follies with detachment, and demanded of me with a sad smile of reproach, "Is this what you *really* want?" I was frank enough with myself to admit that it wasn't.

Gradually the longing grew within me to stop wasting time. I could see that there was too much in life to learn, too much towards which to grow. For my English source theme at the end of the school year I elected to write on the subject, *The Different Concepts of the Universe that Were Held by Ancient Civilizations, and the Quality in Each Civilization that Influenced the Development of Its Particular Concept.* Questions that had no part in my Great Experiment returned insistently to my mind: What is life? What is the universe? What is the purpose of life on earth? Such issues could not be laughed away with another night at Nick's.

One evening a classmate and I visited a local diner, an "in" place with the high school crowd. While we were waiting for seats, my friend began making impromptu additions to the music that was playing on the juke box. Laughingly I encouraged him. All the while, however, my silent inner "friend" demanded of me indignantly, "What is all this jerking about, this nodding of the head up and down like an animated puppet, this contortion of the facial muscles? Is not this, too, a kind of drunkenness?"

My outer friend wrote afterwards in my year book how much he had enjoyed our little "jam session" together. But I felt merely embarrassed by it, as though I had been the plaything of a rhythm-induced hysteria.

At Scarsdale High I learned that I could, if I wanted to, play the Great American Popularity Game and come out, in a sense, a winner. But my success had not made me any happier. If I felt that I now understood something of what other young people wanted from life, I couldn't say that I was any more attracted to their vision.

I was back almost at the beginning. The one thing I had learned this year was how to wrap a veil around myself and hide my true feelings. Well, perhaps after all this was a useful lesson. There can be little merit in exposing one's highest aspirations to people who don't appreciate them. But it wasn't much of a step towards *fulfilling* my aspirations. My next step, I realized, must be more deliberately in the direction of that fulfillment.

Chapter Seven

To Thine Own Search Be True

I GRADUATED FROM Scarsdale High School in June, 1943, shortly after turning seventeen. Bob and I were invited by George Calvert, a school friend of ours, to work with him on his father's farm in upstate New York. That summer we picked strawberries and pitched hay. The work was vigorous, healthful, and good fun. After six or seven weeks as a farm hand, I decided to take advantage of my vacation to broaden my experience of the world. The change I hit upon was radical: from bucolic pastures to grey skyscrapers and acres of sterile concrete.

New York! I worked there as a messenger boy for the *Herald Tribune*. Every day, dodging determined cars, trucks, and buses, and weaving through impatient hordes of shoppers, my fellow messenger boys and I visited the inner sanctums of well-known department stores, delivered advertising copy to and from countless corporations, and swept pellmell through the rushing bloodstream of big-city life. The myriad sense impressions were stimulating, almost overwhelming. In madly bobbing faces on crowded sidewalks, in pleading glances from behind drugstore counters, in fleeting smiles, frosty stares, angry gestures, twitching lips, and self-preoccupied frowns, I saw mankind in virtual caricature, exaggerated out of all credible proportion by the sheer enormity of numbers. Here were tumbling waves of humanity: the youthfully exuberant, the sad and lonely, the stage-struck, the grimly success-oriented, the hard and cynical, the fragile, the lost. All looked hurried and nervous. All seemed harassed by desire.

New York! Its heaving sea of humanity charms and repels in the same instant. It encourages a sense of exaggerated self-importance in those who pride themselves on living in one of the largest, most vital cities in the world. But, in the anonymity it imposes on its faceless millions, it also mocks at self-importance. New Yorkers face a perennial conflict between these opposing challenges to their egos, a conflict that is resolved only by those who seek a broader, spiritual identity. For in the frenzied pace of big-city life it is as if God were whispering to the soul: "Dance with bubbles if you like, but when you tire of dancing, and your bubbles begin bursting one by one, look about you at all these other faces. They are your spiritual brothers and sisters, mirrors to your own self! They *are* you. O little wave, transcend your littleness. Be one with all of them. Be one with life!"

When autumn came I began my higher education at Haverford College, a small men's college on the Main Line to Paoli from Philadelphia. At that time, owing to the war, it was smaller than ever.

The students were bright-eyed, enthusiastic, and intelligent; the professors, quiet, sedate, seriously concerned for their students' welfare. Haverford, a Quaker college, conveys the simple, serene dignity that is to be expected of institutions run by that pacific sect. I don't mean we students didn't have our normal boys' share of high times, but these were always inflicted on a background of gentle disapproval from the discreet greystone-and-ivy buildings, and of restrained dismay from our ever-concerned faculty.

The diminished student body was composed mostly of freshmen, a fact which didn't conduce greatly to the maintenance of certain hallowed college traditions, such as freshmen hazing. When a handful of upperclassmen appeared one day in our dormitory to subject us to that ancient rite, we met them with another venerable American institution: the bum's rush. With whoops of joy, flying pillows, energetic shoves, and a solid phalanx of inverted chairs, we drove them down the stairs and out of the building. Thereafter they left us strictly alone, concluding, no doubt, that in wartime there are certain sacrifices which older and wiser heads must make in the name of peace.

We freshman were so dominant numerically

The Search

that I actually made the football team. One of my problems at Scarsdale High, apart from my light weight, had been that I could never throw the ball properly; my hands were simply too small to get a grip on it. At Haverford our coach, "Pop" Haddleton, solved this problem by making me a running guard. Counting on speed rather than weight, I found I could pull larger opponents off balance while they were still shifting their bodies into position to block me. I would then dash through the line and catch many a runner before he'd got off to a good start with the ball. The left guard, a boy named Mason, was as lightweight as I. Our college newspaper was soon dubbing us "the watch charm guards."

My big play of the season came near the end of a game. Up to that point neither team had scored. In a last, desperate maneuver we were going to try an end run down half the length of the field. I was to run interference. We cleared the end safely, and were well on our way into "enemy territory," when two men rushed to intercept us. I prepared to block the first of them, hoping our runner would be able to dodge the second. Just then I tripped on a dangling shoelace! Sprawling full length onto the ground, I made a perfect, though involuntary, double block. Our man went on to make the touchdown. And I was the hero of the hour. I tried to explain what had really happened, but no one wanted to believe me.

We won every game that season. And so it was that my school athletic career reached a happy climax — before petering out altogether.

For not long after this, college sports and I came to a rather cool parting of the ways. Our separation was due partly to my increasing preoccupation with the search for meaning, and partly, I'm afraid, to the fact that I was attaching "meaning" to a few of the wrong things — like sitting in local bars with friends, nursing a variety of poisonous decoctions, and talking philosophy into the wee hours.

I began devoting much of my free time also to writing poetry, the themes of which related to questions that had long been bothering me: Why suffering? Why warfare and destruction? How is it that God countenances hatred and other forms of human madness? Surely, I thought, suffering can't be His *will* for us? Must it not be a sign, rather, that man is *out of harmony* with God's will?

And what of eternal life? Not even matter or energy can be destroyed. Was it not reasonable, then, to suppose that life, too, is eternal? And if eternal, what about heaven and hell? I wrote a poem at this time in which I postulated a world after death that is perceived differently by each individual, seeming to be either beautiful or ugly, happy or sad, according to the state of consciousness he brings with him from this world.

At this point in my life I might easily have embraced a religious calling. But I knew too little about it, and found no guidance from others in directions that were meaningful to me. Haverford College is a prominent center of Quakerism. In my time there, leading members of this society were on the faculty: Douglas Steere, Rufus Jones, Howard Comfort. I was impressed by their transparent earnestness and goodness. I also liked the Quaker practice of sitting quietly in meditation at the Sunday services —

"meetings," as they were called. Above all, I liked the Quakers for their simplicity. All that they did seemed admirable to me. But somehow I could find no challenge in it. I was seeking a path that would engross me utterly, not one that I could contemplate benignly while puffing on a pipe.

Sunday meetings became all too frequently the scene of genteel competition. The Quakers have no ordained ministers; their members sit in silence on Sunday mornings until one of them feels moved "of the Spirit" to rise and share some inspiration with others. Haverford being an intellectual community, our Sunday meetings were more than usually taken up with this kind of "moving." Hardly a minute passed in silence before someone else was on his feet, sharing with everyone else. Sometimes two or more were moved simultaneously — though, in such cases, courtesy always prevailed.

I'll never forget Douglas Steere rising one day to inquire brightly, "Is there a little bird in your bosom?" Involuntarily my hand went to my chest. The solemnity of the occasion, and my own respect for him, prevented me from succumbing to hilarity on the spot, but afterward my friends and I made up delightedly for our heroic repression.

Doubtless I had much to learn, not the least being reverence and humility. It may be that those religious leaders had more to teach me than I knew. But since I didn't know it, I had no choice but to follow my own star.

Early during my first semester at Haverford I made friends with Julius Katchen, who later acquired fame as a concert pianist in Europe. I loved his intensity and enthusiasm. And though I was less agreeably impressed by his egotism, I found compensation for it in his romantic devotion to every form of art, music, and poetry. Our friendship flourished in the soil of kindred artistic interests. In this relationship, Julius was the musician, and I, the poet. Through our association my feelings for poetry became more musical, artistically more romantic. Julius's mother, too, had been a concert pianist. When I visited the Katchen home in Long Branch, New Jersey, I was caught up in his entire family's devotion to the arts.

At this time, also, I took a course in poetry composition at nearby Bryn Mawr College under the famous poet, W. H. Auden. Auden encouraged me in my poetic efforts. For some time thereafter, poetry became my god.

Yet there was another side of me that could not remain satisfied for long with Keats's romantic fiction, "Truth is beauty, beauty, truth." In every question, what mattered most to me was not whether an idea was beautiful, but whether in some much deeper sense it was *true*. In this concern I found myself increasingly out of tune with the approach our professors took, which was to view all intellectual commitment with suspicion. Scholarly detachment, not commitment, was their guiding principle.

"That's all very well," I would think. "I want to be objective, too. But I don't want to spend my life sitting on a fence. Even objectivity ought to lead one to conclusions of *some* kind." To my professors, scholarly detachment meant holding a perennial question mark up to life. It meant supporting, "for the sake of discussion," positions to which they didn't really subscribe. It meant showing equal interest in every argument, without endorsing any. I was impatient with their indecisiveness.

My need for truths to which I could commit myself had posed a problem for me in our debating society at Kent School. It made me a failure in public speaking classes during my freshman year at Haverford, and a bad actor in the plays in which I occasionally took part, during college and afterward. It ruined my chances, years later, as a radio announcer. More and more it was to give me difficulties as a student as well, particularly in such subjects as English literature and philosophy. I *had* to know whether what we were considering was true. In reaction against my professors and their insistence on a spirit of polite scholarly inquiry, I gradually developed a rebellious attitude toward college in general.

It was at about this time that I met a student at Haverford whose search for truth coincided more nearly with my own. Rod Brown was two years older than I, exceedingly intelligent, and a gifted poet. At first our relationship was one of learned sage and unlettered bumpkin of a disciple. Rod treated me with a certain amused condescension, as the ingenuous youngster that I was. My poems he read tolerantly, never lavishing higher praise on them than to call them "nice." *His* poems I couldn't even understand. He would quote at length from countless books I'd never heard of, and could make each quotation sound so important that one got the impression that only a confirmed ignoramus would dare to face life without at least the ability to paraphrase that passage.

Rod was a sensitive young man who had learned early in life to fend off others' rejection of him by treating them with disdain. It was purely a defense mechanism, but he carried it off well. I was as intrigued by his superior attitude towards me for my ignorance as I was captivated by his single-minded devotion to philosophical realities. Surely, I thought, if he knew enough to look down on me, it behooved me to learn what the view was from his altitude.

In time we became fast friends. I discovered that, besides his enthusiasm for truth, he had a delightful sense of humor, and was eager to share his ideas and opinions, always fresh and interesting, with others. Rod only raised a supercilious eyebrow at my theories about God, suffering, and eternal life. Rhetorically he would ask, "How can anyone ever know the answers to such questions?" But he directed my thinking constructively into more immediate channels. For the time being the quest for religious truths dropped out of my life. But where the search concerns truth, can *true* religion be very far away?

Indeed, Rod's thinking and mine verged constantly on the spiritual. He introduced me to Emerson and Thoreau. I drank eagerly at the fountain of wisdom in "The Over-Soul," in "Self-Reliance," and in *Walden*. These writings were the closest I had come so far to the expansive vistas of Indian thought,* for though I didn't realize it at the time,

---

*In those days, courses in Indian studies were comparatively rare. The only actual exposure I ever got to them was from Douglas Steere,

Emerson and Thoreau were both admirers of India's Scriptures, and echoed in their own writings the lofty teachings of the *Upanishads* and the *Bhagavad Gita*.

Rod prompted me to stop concerning myself with life's meaning as an abstraction, and to face the more concrete problem of how to live wisely among men. One of the principles we discussed night after night was nonattachment. Another was the courage to reject values that we considered false, even if all other men believed in them. Amusing as it seems now, we spent hours discussing intellectually the uselessness of intellectualism. And, deciding that the uneducated masses were surely more genuine than we in their simple, earthy attitudes, we set out with pioneering zeal to frequent the haunts of truck drivers and manual laborers. No deep wisdom was ever born of these outings, but then, people who hold cherished theories rarely feel a need to sustain them on the coarse fare of facts!

Not everything Rod said or did won my support. He told me approvingly, for instance, of an older friend of his who had an unnaturally small heart. To Rod and his friend this fact suggested a lack of emotional capacity, and, therefore, a nature truly nonattached. But I disagreed with their equation, for I considered nonattachment and feeling not at all incompatible with each other. The important point, rather, I felt, was that one's feelings be *impersonal*. Nonattachment releases one from identity

in his freshman course on the history of philosopy. For the first twenty minutes of his first class Dr. Steere touched lightly on the *Vedas*, giving us the impression, merely, that there *was* such a thing as Indian philosophy.

with a mere handful of things, and should therefore permit an *expansion*, and *increase*, of feeling.

Rod also believed that, armed with a genuine spirit of nonattachment, one could behave in as worldly a manner as one pleased. But this argument struck me as too convenient a rationalization for his own worldliness. For Rod, despite his disdain for middle-class values and his praise of lower-class simplicity, betrayed a marked fondness for upper-class luxuries. Though he often mocked me for my innocence, I myself looked upon innocence as a truer safeguard of nonattachment.

Rod, like all men, had his shortcomings. He was, among other things, somewhat intolerant of disagreement, proud of his own brilliance, and unabashedly lazy. But for all that he was at heart a loving and true friend, deeply concerned about countless others despite his vaunted indifference, more hurt by people's rejection of him than honestly disdainful of them in return, and a great deal more conservative in his values than he would ever have admitted. While others clucked disapprovingly at him, I saw him as one person who could really help me to think boldly for myself. For this reason above all, I was grateful for his friendship.

Yet in my association with him I also acquired some of the very traits I disapproved of in him. Such, indeed, is the power of all human association. Like Rod, I developed intellectual pride as a defense against rejection and misunderstanding. Perhaps worst of all, I acquired some of his worldliness, though never so much so that Rod ceased to twit me for what he called my naiveté.

The Search

In those days it was Rod who gave me my real education. My classes formed a mere backdrop; they taught me facts, but in discussions with him I learned what I would do with facts. Night after night we sat discussing life over pots of coffee in our rooms, or in bars, or in an off-campus restaurant with the engaging name, "The Last Straw." We had few friends, but that no longer really mattered to me. I was seeking truth now, not the mere opinions of men.

My cousin Bet, at Wellesley College, Massachusetts

My college friend, Rod Brown, and I in Wellesley, Massachusetts

Our Haverford football team —
I am in the front row, third from left

As a monk at Mount Washington, in 1951

Chapter Eight

Joy Is the Goal

MY FIRST YEAR AT Haverford was one of joyous sifting of new ideas. During my second year there, I tried to digest those ideas and make them my own. The digestive process took place on two levels, the one abstract, and the other deeply personal.

On the abstract level, association with Rod had coaxed me out of my former preoccupation with suffering, and with the essential unreality of this world. I was beginning to see the world more affirmatively. Even suffering seemed to me conquerable now, by the simple — and perhaps simplistic — expedient of strong, positive affirmation.

On the personal level, I was learning to affirm my own worth, a worth I had doubted during my years at Hackley and Kent, then affirmed artificially at Scarsdale High. Now, at Haverford, in the company of friends who shared many of my ideals, I was discovering in myself a basis for genuine self-acceptance.

Once I had somewhat digested my new attitudes, my two-fronts advance converged on a single point. For both abstract and personal reasons, I began to find myself able to express once again that most battered of virtues: trust. In the words of Emerson, I was beginning to feel that the world was my "oyster," that life was basically sunny, right, and beautiful. Even the disapproval of worldly people could no longer dampen my expanding trust in life, and, on a certain level, in them. For I felt they merely lacked the courage to live up to a truth which, deep in their hearts, they believed in. I longed for the power to bring them joy.

Trust! This joyful offering I now made to life was selfless and pure. Yet the wise have ever said that one should trust fully only in God, that to place faith in earthly accomplishments is like expecting perpetual stability of a ship at sea. Alas, I hadn't their wisdom to guide me. All my faith now I flung with ardent enthusiasm into the fragile basket of this world.

For my sophomore year I was assigned to a suite in Lloyd Hall, which in normal times was reserved for upper classmen. My roommate was from Argentina. Roberto Pablo Payro was his name; I understand he has since become a successful novelist in his country. Roberto was quiet, dignified, and ever courteous: ideal qualities in a roommate. We got along well together, though the goals we pursued were different. Roberto's social life was as quiet as he was. He liked sophisticated, serious discussions, mostly on such down-to-earth subjects as politics and sociology, and rather marveled that such abstractions as "life" and "truth" could command from me the intense enthusiasm that they did. My tendency was to seize a thought firmly, wrestle with it for days until I felt I'd mastered it, and then to dash out, laughing, in search of friends with whom I could celebrate my victory. To Roberto I must have seemed alternately far too intense, and inconsistently frivolous.

But thought itself was, for me, a joyous adventure. It was only years later, after I met my guru, that I learned that thinking is but a by-path to truth, and that the highest perceptions are possible only when the fluctuations of the mind have been stilled.

Rod was the best friend I had found so far in this country. We spent much time together, continuing our nocturnal rounds of coffee, drinks, and wee-hour philosophizing. But I was beginning also to spend more time now seeking truth on my own.

For my college major I selected English literature. I loved reading the great works that comprise our true heritage — a heritage of insights and inspiration, not of mere worldly accomplishments. Reading Shakespeare, Donne, and numerous others, I pondered a new question: In what ways has great literature served the cause of truth? As an aspiring writer myself, I hoped to make whatever I wrote serve as an instrument of the highest vision.

But there was buoyant good humor, too, in our seeking. Rod and I could laugh merrily over the gravest of issues. A few somber souls there were who viewed our unconventional levity with dismay. I think they considered it a proof that we were dissolute, misspending our youth in drunkenness and debauchery. But we had little patience with people who equated seriousness with joylessness. Taking my cue from Rod, I would sometimes delight in pretending we were in league with forces unspeakably dark. (The effort to imagine such forces I left entirely to our critics!)

One of our fellow students, with the appropriate last name of Coffin, used to carry a Bible around with him wherever he went, the more sadly to reproach anyone who showed a disposition occasionally to kick up his heels. "The wages of sin," Coffin would remind us sinners gravely, citing chapter and verse, "is death." As my own reputation for cheerful irreverence spread, he took to bringing me, particularly, the Good News. Entering my room one morning before I'd fairly tested the world to make sure it was still there, he sat on the edge of my bed, the Bible open in his hands, looked at me dolefully, and — sighed.

If only religion weren't made so lugubrious, I think many people might be inspired to seek God who presently confuse ministers with undertakers. It was years before I myself learned that religious worship needn't verge on the funereal — that it can be, as Paramhansa Yogananda put it, the joyous funeral of all sorrows. As it was, I satisfied a natural craving for religious inspiration by laughing at the lack of it in religion as I found it practiced. Had I known better, I might have sincerely worshipped.

During our second year at Haverford someone gave Rod a few guppies in a glass bowl. *Guppy*, we decided, was far too undignified a name even for so nondescript a creature. We renamed his new pets, accordingly, "The Sacred White Fish." Soon, enlarging on this grand concept, we created an entire religion, complete with ceremonies, dogmas, and ritual responses. I even found a partially completed, abandoned chapel for our rites. Needless to say, our comedy never advanced beyond the playful planning stage, but we had great fun with it.

One day Rod was summoned into the dean's office. "What's this I hear, Mr. Brown," began Mr. Gibb cautiously, "about — ah — how shall I put it? — a new religion? Something about the — ah — sacred — ah — white — ah — *fish*? Have I heard this incredible tale correctly?" We never learned whom it was we'd shocked into reporting us to the dean, but even this anonymous outrage added fresh zest to our game.

Yet I also felt, inexplicably, a deep, almost wistful thrill at the thought of helping to found a new religion. Perhaps it was because the fun we were having with those guppies underscored for me the joy that I missed in the churches. But to me it was more than fun. My search for truth, and for joy as the very essence of truth, held an almost life-or-death earnestness.

On another matter I felt less keenly the need to cloak my interest under a guise of playfulness. A continuous aspiration of mine since the age of fifteen had been the founding of a "utopian" community. Utopia literally means, "not a place"; the word is generally used to describe any impractical communitarian dream. But I was convinced that an intentional community founded on high ideals could be made viable, with sufficient realism and foresight. During this period at Haverford, and for years thereafter, I devoted considerable time to studying and thinking about the problems connected with such a project. On some deep level I believed it was my duty someday to found such a community.

Among my friends, however, I encountered little sympathy for the idea. When I spoke of it to a few of them, they expressed mild interest, only to lose it altogether when they realized I was completely in earnest. After that, they left me to do my dreaming alone.

Undaunted by their lack of interest, I simply broadened my horizons to include the rest of the human race! The more I thought about intentional communities, the more clearly I saw them not as a step backward into primitive simplicity, but as a step *forward* in social evolution, a natural progression from machine technology and the self-defeating complexity of modern life to a new kind of *enlightened* simplicity, one in which technology served human, nor merely mechanical or economic ends.

Decentralization seemed to me a growing need, too, in this age. The essentially sterile demands for efficiency that are served by centralizing power in big industry and big government would, I believed, be balanced by the human and idealistic values that would be emphasized in small, spiritually integral communities.

With my growing enthusiasm for life I also took increasing pleasure in singing. At last I resolved to take singing lessons. Dr. Frederick Schlieder, the noted pianist and organist, recommended to Mother that I study under Marie Zimmerman, a singing teacher in Philadelphia. "She is a real musician," he assured Mother. "Your son is fortunate to be in college so nearby."

One day I took a train into Philadelphia and visited Mrs. Zimmerman in her studio. Seventy-five years old she must have been at that time. A concert singer in her younger days, her voice, now no longer beautiful, was still perfectly placed.

"The voice," she explained to me, "is an instrument that can't be seen. I can't *show* you how to use it, as I could how to play the piano. You'll have to listen sensitively as I sing a note, then try to imitate the sound that I make. The more perceptively you listen, the more quickly you'll learn."

Next she placed my right hand over her stomach. "I'm going to show you how to breathe properly," she explained. As she inhaled, her diaphragm moved downward, pushing the stomach out. I prepared to listen to a full, operative tone.

"Mooooooooooo!" came the feeble croak, its sound hardly powerful enough to fill a pantry, let alone a concert hall. I fought to suppress my mirth.

But her voice *was* well placed. Recalling Dr. Schlieder's high recommendations, I decided to study with her.

"You will pay me five dollars a lesson," she announced firmly.

"It isn't that I need the money. I don't. But *you*

need to pay it. It will help you to take your lessons seriously."

I didn't want to bother Dad for the weekly fees, so I took a job waiting on tables one night a week at The Last Straw. From those earnings I paid for my lessons.

Maria Zimmerman proved an excellent teacher. Unlike most voice teachers, she wouldn't let me sing on my own for the first weeks. Gradually only, as my placement improved, she allowed me to practice a little at home, then a little bit more. The farther I progressed, the more I grew to enjoy these lessons, until at last they became the high point of my week.

Marie Zimmerman was not only an excellent teacher and a fine musician; she was also a remarkable woman. Deeply, calmly religious, she was content with only the highest and noblest in everything. She was, in fact, an impressive example of a truth that was becoming increasingly clear to me, that the chief masterpiece of an aspiring artist must be *himself*.

One day at about this time I had what was, to me, a revelation. Sudden, vivid, and intense, it gave me in the space of a few minutes insights into the nature of art, and of art's relationship to truth, that have guided my thinking ever since.

The word *art*, as Rod and I used it, encompassed *all* the creative arts including music and literature. We had pondered authorities whose claim was that art should be for art's sake alone; or that it must capture reality as a camera does, literally; or that it ought to reflect a sense of social responsibility; or be a purely personal catharsis; or express the spirit of the times in which the artist lives.

Suddenly I felt certain of a truth deeper than all of these. Most artistic theories, I realized, emphasize primarily the *forms* of art. But art is essentially a human, not an abstract phenomenon. A man's intrinsic worth is determined not by his physical appearance, but by his spirit, his essential attitudes, his courage or cowardice, his wisdom or ignorance. With art, similarly, it is the artist's vision of life, not his medium of expression, that determines the validity of his work. Inspiration, or sterility: Either can be expressed as well through realism as through impressionism. The essential question is: *How great does the artist's work reveal HIM to be, as a man?* Only if *he* is great will his work stand a chance of being truly great also. Otherwise it may reveal superlative craftsmanship, but lest plumbers, too, deserve acceptance as artists, mere skill cannot serve to define art.*

My first task as a writer, I decided, was no different from my first task as a human being. It was to determine what constitutes ideal human qualities, and then to try to develop *myself* accordingly.

At about this time we were given the assignment in English class of writing an essay on our personal criteria of greatness in literature. Not feeling competent as yet to explain some of the subtler nuances of my revelation, I confined myself to one aspect of it — one perhaps subtler than all the rest! I wrote that, after reading Homer's *Iliad*, I had sensed a blazing white light emanating from it. Later, as I

---

*Meaning in the arts is the subject of my book titled *The Artist as a Channel* (Crystal Clarity, Publishers, 1987).

contemplated other great works, I had sensed again in each case a bright light, though in no case so intense as Homer's. Chaucer's light seemed of a duller hue than Milton's, Dante's or Shakespeare's. From still lesser works I sensed no light at all; it was as though they were spiritually dead. I admitted that I saw no objective reason for giving Homer the highest marks; his epic seemed to me, on the surface, only a good, rousing war story. But I knew from its light that it must be a work of superlative greatness.*

My poor professor! Shaking his head in bewilderment, he gave me a flunking grade. Yet even today I consider the criterion of greatness that I described in that paper to have been just and valid.

Rod and I continued our discussions on philosophical matters: intellectual integrity, for example, and living in the *now*, and the importance of nonattachment. Nonattachment, I was coming to realize, is crucial to human happiness. No one can truly enjoy what he fears to lose.

One evening my nonattachment was put to an unusual test. I was sitting in my bedroom, studying for a philosophy exam. The textbook was exceptionally dull. Midway through my study, as I was reflecting glumly that this author valued pedantry over clarity, I heard footsteps approaching stealthily over the dry leaves on the ground outside my window. I glanced at my watch. Nine-thirty: the hour the library closed. One of my friends must be planning to play a joke on me on his way back from

---

*Homer was customarily referred to by ancient Greeks as *"divine* Homer."

there. Smiling, I stepped over to the window to show him I'd caught him at his little game.

At once the footsteps fled into the night. Whoever it was would, I assumed with a smile, come around through the front door and we'd enjoy a friendly chuckle before he returned to his own room.

To my surprise, no one came.

Smiling at the improbable fancy, I thought, "Maybe someone wanted to shoot me!"

Twenty minutes passed. Again the footsteps came, this time even more softly over the dead leaves.

Who could it be? My friends weren't this persistent at *anything*! Perhaps it really *was* someone wanting to shoot me. Silently I stepped to the window. Once again the steps faded hastily into the darkness.

By this time my curiosity was thoroughly aroused. How would I ever know who this mysterious intruder was, or what he wanted, if I persisted in frightening him off? If he returned a third time, I decided, I would pretend I hadn't heard him.

Another twenty minutes passed. Finally once again: footsteps, this time more stealthy than ever. Moments later, a shoe scraped lightly on the ledge below my window. A hand grasped the metal grating over the window.

Suppressing a smile, I kept my eyes glued on the page before me.

Suddenly: an ear-splitting shot! For several seconds I heard nothing but the ringing in my ears; then, gradually, the ticking clock on my dresser; a car in the nearest parking lot revved its motor and roared off the campus at high speed.

Amazed, I leaned back in my chair and — laughed delightedly! It seemed incredible that such a thing could have actually happened. I checked my body: No holes anywhere. No blood. No pain. What? *Nothing* to show for this absurd adventure? I stepped over to examine the window. The screen was intact. What did it all mean?

Days later I learned that that evening had been Halloween! Evidently some village boy had decided, as a Halloween prank, to put the fear of God into a college student. He'd fired a blank cartridge!

I knew one ought to show a greater sense of responsibiliity toward one's body than I had. But I was happy at least to have had this experience as evidence of some definite measure of my nonattachment.

Soon, however, I received another test of my nonattachment, and this one I didn't pass so easily. It was a test of my developing ability to offer trust unreservedly.

Haverford boys usually dated Bryn Mawr girls. I did too, whenever I had the inclination for it — and the money, which was seldom. I finally met a girl at Bryn Mawr named Sue, who came to epitomize for me everything that was good, kind, and holy in life. Her tastes were simple. Her smile expressed so much sweetness that, whether blindly or with actual insight, I could not imagine her holding a mean thought. Our joy in each other's company was such that we never felt the need to go anywhere in particular. A quiet walk through green fields, a friendly chat, a communion of hearts in precious silence:

These were the essence of a relationship more beautiful than any I had ever before known.

I had no thought of marriage, of long years spent together, or of anything, really, beyond the present. Sue was for me not so much a girlfriend as a symbol of my new gift for trust, for giving myself to life joyously, without the slightest thought of return. How she felt toward me seemed almost irrelevant. It was enough, I felt, that my own love for her was true.

Yet there were times, in the happiness of moments together, when she would gaze at me sadly. She wouldn't say why. "Never mind," I would think, "I will only give her the more love, until all her sadness is washed away."

For Christmas vacation I went home. Shortly after the New Year I received a letter from Sue. Eagerly I tore it open.

"Dear Don," it began, "there is something I've been needing to tell you. I realize I should have done so early in our friendship, but I enjoyed your company and didn't want to lose it." She went on to say how deeply she had come to feel about me, and how sad also, that the realities of her life were such that she could never see me again. She was married, she explained, and was even then carrying her husband's baby. Her husband was stationed overseas in the navy. She had realized she would not be allowed to return to college once it became known she was pregnant; hence her resolution of silence. But she had been feeling increasingly unhappy about this resolution insofar as I was concerned. She realized she should have had the courage to tell me sooner. Now she would not be returning to Bryn

Mawr to finish the school year. She hoped I would understand the loneliness that had motivated her to go out with me. She had never wanted to hurt me, and was unhappy in the knowledge that such a hurt now was inevitable.

The effect of her letter was devastating. I didn't blame Sue, but rather sympathized with the predicament she'd been in. I reminded myself that I had never asked her to return my love, that in fact I'd never contemplated marriage to anyone. But, oh, the pain! And had I, I asked myself, been wrong to trust so completely?

Put differently, was the whole structure of my inner development, in which trust played so vital a role, made of sand?

Much time was to pass before I understood that life, without God, is *never* trustworthy. It is not earthly fulfillment that deserves our faith, but God alone; not outer circumstances, but His inner blessings in the soul. These alone can never fail, can never disappoint. For God is our only true love. Until we learn to place ourselves unreservedly in His hands, our trust, wherever else we give it, will — *must*, indeed — be betrayed again and again.

Can a boat ride calmly in a storm? How can a world in constant flux offer more than delusive security?

For months to come my problem was not disillusionment, for I determined with all my heart to trust life in spite of anything else that might come to hurt me. My problem, rather, was how to find a firm base on which to repose my trust.

I blessed Sue when I received her letter. I bless

her even more now. For through our friendship, and even more through our parting, I was brought closer to God.

Chapter Nine

He Gathers Strength for the Climb

AT ABOUT THIS TIME in my life I had an interesting dream. I was living with many other people in a torture chamber. For generations our families had lived here, knowing no world but this one; the possibility of any other world simply never occurred to us. One awoke, one was tortured, and at night one found brief respite in sleep. What else could there be to life? We didn't particularly mind our lot. Rather, we imagined ourselves reasonably well-off. Oh, there were bad days to be sure, but then there were also good ones — days together, sometimes, when we were less tortured than usual.

The time came, however, when a handful of us began thinking the unthinkable. Might there, we asked ourselves, just possibly be *another*, a better way of life? Moments snatched when our torturers were out of earshot served to kindle our speculations. At last we determined to rebel.

We laid our plans carefully. One day, rising in unison from our tasks, we slew the torturers and escaped. Slipping out of the great room cautiously, lest armies of torturers be waiting for us outside, we encountered no one. The torture chamber itself, it turned out, occupied only the top floor of a large, otherwise empty building. We walked unchallenged down flights of stairs, emerging from the ground floor onto a vast, empty plain. Confined as we'd been all our lives in the torture chamber, the horizon seemed incredibly distant. Joyfully we inhaled the fresh air. Gazing about us, we all but shouted the new word: Freedom!

Before departing the building forever, we glanced upward to the top floor, scene of the only life we'd ever known. There, to our astonishment, were the very torturers we thought we'd slain, going about their business as though nothing had happened! Amazed, we looked to one another for an explanation.

And then the solution dawned on me. "Don't you see?" I cried. "It's ourselves we've conquered, not the torturers!"

With that realization I awoke.

I felt that this dream held an important meaning for me. The prison, located as it had been on the top floor of the building, symbolized for me the human mind. The torturers represented our mental shortcomings. The emptiness of the rest of the building meant to me that once one overcomes his mental torturers, he finds no more enemies left to conquer. All human suffering, in other words, originates in the mind.

My dream, I felt, held a divine message for me. Its implication was that the time had come for me to seek a higher life. But *how* was I to seek it? I knew nothing of great saints who had communed with God. To me this very word, saint, connoted only a person of frail goodness, not one filled with divine love, and certainly not with ecstasy. All I knew of religion were the stylized church services I had attended, the uninspired ministers I had listened to — insecure men who sought support for their faith in the approval of others, not in the unbribable voice of their own conscience.

Though I didn't realize it at the time, my ignorance concerning the spiritual path was my own chief "torturer"; it hindered me from seeking the good for which my soul longed. Subordinate to ignorance there were other, more evident failings — doubt, for example. Had I approached truth by love I might have gone straight to the mark. But I was trying to *think* my way to wisdom. God I looked upon as Something to be thought about, not Someone with whom one could commune. I wanted desperately to trust, even to love, but had no idea what, specifically, to trust or to love. I had reached a point where I thought about God almost constantly; but He remained silent, for I never called to Him.

Another of my mental torturers was fear. Certainly I had never considered myself a fearful person, but that was because in most matters I was nonattached. In one test of my nonattachment, however, I had shown myself exceedingly vulnerable: I feared disappointment from others.

Peace in this world depends on cheerfully relinquishing attachment to all things, even to ego. As long as I strove to protect my sense of personal worth, I would suffer again and again, ever in essentially the same ways.

I was not yet wise enough to see clearly, but at least my vision was improving. My dream about the torture chamber, conveying as it did a sense of divine guidance, had made me more aware of realities beyond those known through the senses. This awareness, coupled with the trust and affirmation that I had worked on developing earlier, led me now to an interesting discovery.

I hit upon what was, as far as I knew then, a novel theory: To be lucky, *expect* luck; don't wait passively for it to come to you, but go out and meet it halfway. With strong, positive expectation, combined with equally positive action, success will be assured. With this simple formula I was to achieve some remarkable results.

Not long after the New Year our first semester ended. At that time Rod, and one or two other friends, flunked out of college. It was hardly surprising, considering the disdain all of us felt for "the system." Their departure put me on my own now in my efforts to understand life more deeply. My independence proved a wholesome opportunity.

I visited Sue's dormitory occasionally, hoping in chats with a few of her friends to relive a little of the happiness I had known with her. But the pain of not finding her there was too keen.

Marie Zimmerman, noticing my low spirits, inquired about them one day. I told her of my little tragedy.

"Ah!" she exclaimed impatiently. "Puppy love! I lived with my husband nearly fifty years. In all that time our friendship kept growing deeper. Since his death we are closer than ever. *That* is love!"

Offended, I told myself she simply didn't understand. But her words remained with me, gently reminding me in my deeper self that I probably had much in life yet to learn.

My college classes had lost all appeal for me. I seldom mixed with the other students. To protect my unhappiness over Sue, I put on an overintellectual front, did frequent battle with words, and assumed an air of self-assurance in which there was considerably more affirmation than self-recognition. My heart was vulnerable, but not my reason or my will.

Mainly, however, I spent my days thinking, thinking, thinking, as if to wrest from life insights into its farthest secrets. Why was the promise of joy so often a will-o'-the-wisp? And was it not essential to a well-ordered universe that love given be in some way returned? Again, where lay the pathway to true happiness?

"Relax!" cried Roberto one day, seeing me staring sightlessly out the window. "Can't you ever relax!"

So the semester passed. In recollection it all seems a grey fog.

My draft board called me for an examination, which I failed because of poor eyesight, thereby resolving the dilemma of whether or not to register as a conscientious objector. I had doubted whether I could register thus in completely good conscience, since it wasn't a matter of my religious convictions; I simply knew with perfect certainty that, even if my own life depended on it, I could never take the life of another human being.

In April, Dad was sent to Rumania as petroleum attaché to the U.S. diplomatic mission in Bucharest.

My job at The Last Straw convinced me, and everyone else (especially my employer!), that whatever my mission in life was, it was not to be a waiter. I kept absent-mindedly sitting down with customers, quite forgetting that there were other tables to be served; then forgetting to change the bill when customers increased their orders. I'm afraid I was almost The Last Straw's last straw!

My singing lessons were the only really bright spot in my life. Marie Zimmerman was a demanding teacher. After six months of weekly lessons she stopped me one day in the midst of a song.

"There!" she cried triumphantly. *"That note. That's how all of them should sound!"*

There were other compensations besides the sheer joy of learning to sing from her. Once she said to me, "If any singing teacher worthy of the name — I mean a real *musician* — were to hear you now, he would be impressed."

And toward the end of the college year, she told me softly, "I am living for only one thing now: to see you become a *great* singer! It isn't only your voice; others have good voices, too. But you have a mind; you *understand.*

The Search

Dear Marie! (May I call you that, now that you've left this world? To call you Mrs. Zimmerman seems too formal when addressing your soul.) How sad I have been that I had to disappoint you. That was our last class together. I *couldn't* go back to you. I knew that to be a singer, even a world-renowned one, was not at all my calling. But maybe you are pleased with the fact that I *have* touched people with my gift — not for money, but for love. And maybe someday, too, if we meet in heaven, or in some other life on earth, I can sing for you again. One of my deepest prayers on the spiritual path has been that all whom I have ever loved be blessed with divine peace and joy. May you be so blessed also.

As the college year began drawing to a close, my prolonged inattention to the daily class routine brought me to a rather awkward predicament. Most of my courses I was at least confident of passing, though barely. Greek, however, was a downright embarrassment. It became a standard joke in class to see whether I would recognize one, or two, Greek words in a paragraph when called upon to translate. The entire semester I did hardly three assignments. As we prepared for the final exam, Dr. Post, our professor, remarked more than once, "Not everyone in this room need trouble himself to appear for that event." Whenever he said this, the other students glanced at me and laughed.

But I determined to show up for the exam, and to pass it. It might take a bit of luck not to flunk, but then, I reminded myself, I also had my new theory on how to attract luck: *Expect* to be lucky, then meet luck halfway with a vigorous, positive attitude.

Unfortunately, I felt anything but vigorous and positive towards the one activity that really mattered: study. A week before the test I finally picked up the textbook and glanced half-heartedly at the first page. It was no use. Giving up, I flung the book aside. "Tomorrow," I consoled myself, "I'll study *twice* as long as I was going to today." But the next day my good intentions were again routed ignominiously. For the rest of the week I showed persistence only in my continued willingness to procrastinate.

Almost before I knew it, the last evening was upon me. And I hadn't studied at all! Even now I fully intended to pass, but I can't imagine anyone in his right mind endorsing these roseate expectations.

Necessity, it is said, is the mother of invention. Fortunately for me, my present extremity displayed the right, maternal instinct. Out of the blue an inspiration appeared.

"You are a Greek," I told myself with all the concentration I could muster, adjusting myself resolutely to this new identity. The results were astonishing.

As an American, I had found the study of Greek difficult. But now as a Greek "my own" language came surprisingly easily. Through some subtle channel in the network of consciousness that binds all men together, I felt myself suddenly in tune with Greek ways of thinking and speaking. Approaching this new language as an old friend, moreover, I no longer faced the age-old problem of the student who, while attracting knowledge with one half of his mind, pushes it away with the other half by his unwillingness to learn. My entire mental flow was in one direction. For two hours I absorbed Greek grammar and vocabulary like a dry sponge in water, until I could hold no more.

The following morning, "Mother Necessity" gave birth to another inspiration. Our class had been studying the New Testament in the original Greek. Dr. Post had told us that we'd be asked to translate a portion of it into English. This morning, then, mindful of my theory on attracting luck, it occurred to me to turn to the King James translation of the Bible. Only enough time remained for me to read one chapter, but if my luck held, this would be the chapter from which the passage would be selected.

It was! The exam that year as it turned out was exceptionally difficult: Only two students passed it. But my theory on luck was vindicated: I was one of them.

From this experience I learned several useful lessons: for one, the mind's power for positive accomplishment, once it learns to resist its own "no"-saying tendency. Much, indeed, of what people do amounts to pushing simultaneously on opposite sides of a door. Working themselves to exhaustion, they yet accomplish little, or nothing. If they would only learn to say "Yes!" to life with all the conviction of their being, their capacity for success might be expanded almost to infinity.

This discovery of the latent power within me, and within every man, was important for me, but even so its interest was secondary to another problem that eluded me still: the secret of happiness.

Is not joy, I asked myself, what all men are really seeking, in their heart of hearts? Why, then, do so few experience it? And why is it so common for people to suffer in the very pursuit of happiness? Toward the end of the semester it occurred to me that perhaps the fault lay with our life-style in America. How, I asked myself, could anyone find true happiness while satiating himself on physical comforts? Thoreau's statement in *Walden* impressed me: "of a life of luxury the fruit is luxury." For the materialist, the heights of inspiration are unimaginable. The worst disease of modern life, I concluded, is complacency. True joy is ever creative; it demands fresh, vital, *intense* awareness. How, I thought impatiently, will happiness worthy of the name ever be felt by people who are too complacent to hold an unconventional thought? Materialism cannot buy happiness.

It is not unusual for this kind of judgment to be met with indulgent smiles, as though the sheer frequency with which it is made, by young people especially, rendered it invalid. But considering the fact that it is arrived at more or less independently by so many seekers after honest values, I think it might be wise to ponder whether it contains an element of truth.

At any rate, my own solution that year to the shortcomings I identified with life in America was to travel abroad. I imagined people in less industrialized countries turning to their daily tasks with a song on their lips, and inspiration in their hearts. Mexico was such a country. I would spend my summer vacation there among simple, happy, spontaneous, *genuine* human beings.

Getting there was my first problem. If I took a job to earn the money for the journey, my vacation might end before I'd saved enough. How, then — short of robbing a bank — could I "get rich quick"? What was called for, obviously, was another application of my theory on luck.

Affirming a bright, positive attitude, I cast about hopefully for a solution. Our college yearbook, I remembered, offered cash prizes for a variety of literary contributions. If only I could win a large enough prize, my problem would be solved! I leafed through the book. Most of the prizes listed were small: ten, fifteen, twenty-five dollars. But then a more promising figure caught my eye: one hundred dollars! This amount would take me far, indeed. Eagerly I checked to see what I must do to win it. Then my heart sank. The requirement was for an essay on the subject, "The Basic Principles Underlying the Government of the United States." Some law professor, probably, dreamed up this legal gem! Why, I thought with a sigh, must educators continually place the highest price on the driest matter? Who would ever write on such a ponderous subject?

I was about to pass on to other prospects when the answering thought came: "That's right: Who *would*?" Examining the information more closely, I found no one listed as having won this prize the previous year. I checked several earlier yearbooks: None of them showed a winner. Perhaps after all there *was* hope! Ignorant though I was of the fine legal or historical points implied in the topic, if mine was the sole entry ...

Anyway, I reflected, I wasn't *completely* ignorant. At least I knew America's basic principles as they are popularly defined: *Life, liberty, and the pursuit of happiness.* That brief phrase might not make much of an essay, but what if I took a fresh approach to it? Would the judges decide I'd skirted the issue if, for example, I examined our present-day society in the light of how truly it was living up to those principles? Here at least I'd be walking familiar ground.

Dividing my essay into three chapters — "Life," "Liberty," and, "The Pursuit of Property" — I sought to demonstrate how, by our relentless acquisitiveness, we were depriving ourselves of all three of our basic rights: life and liberty, as well as happiness.

My paper was the sole entry. It won the prize.

Another prize offered in the yearbook was of fifteen dollars for the best poem submitted. Though this was hardly "big money," it seemed worth a light stab; I already had a few poems written that I could submit. In this effort, I knew, I faced competition. The campus poetry club had been debating which of its members would walk away with the prize; they'd already made clear their view that I, who wasn't a member, didn't stand a chance. In the past we'd crossed swords on the subject of solitary, versus group, creativity. To me a poetry *club* seemed a contradiction in terms. I saw it as a victory for my own point of view when this prize came to me.

Thus, with $115 in my pocket before the vacation had even started, I decided I had enough money for the journey. If I found later that I needed more,

Lady Luck would no doubt provide it. Barely nineteen years old, never before on my own, and with my parents far away in Rumania: I considered myself an adventurer indeed!

Before leaving for Mexico, I took a short trip north to Massachusetts to visit Rod. Soon thereafter my great odyssey began. Heading south, I made use of a return-trip train ticket that I was holding from New York to Philadelphia. From Philadelphia I planned to hitchhike, armed with my so-far-successful formula for attracting luck, and burdened with nothing but a knapsack.

A young couple seated behind me in the train noticed the knapsack, and engaged me in conversation. Was I a hiker? They themselves were enthusiastic youth hostelers. We chatted pleasantly; soon we were singing folk songs. By the time we reached Philadelphia we felt like old friends. They invited me to spend the night in their family home in Ardmore, the town before Haverford on the main line.

This home turned out to be no mere residence, but a veritable mansion. Their hospitality, too, was extraordinary. A member of the family was about to be married; relatives were arriving from distant parts. Food fit for the most educated tastes was being served at every meal. Lady Luck, I reflected, seemed particularly well disposed towards me!

The following morning, as I was sitting in the living room preparatory to leaving, the dowager of the clan entered and took a chair next to mine. Her smiling manner hinted at good news for me.

"I have a nephew," she began, "who is being sent

by his firm to Mexico City. He will be leaving tomorrow by car. As he is traveling alone, I'm sure he would appreciate company. Do you think you might like to go with him?"

A three-thousand-mile ride! Lady Luck was taking a most welcome interest in my case. Bob Watson, the nephew, not only took me along, but appointed me his extra driver, thereby paying all my travel expenses from his expense account. When we reached Mexico City, he put me up in his home. Thus my money, which I found had less purchasing power than I'd imagined, lasted me the entire summer.

Bob, and later his wife Dorothy when she joined us, were the kindest of friends to me. Our Mexican adventure was as new and fascinating for them as it was for me. Together we shared its daily lessons, rewards, and comic twists as we reported our new experiences to one another in the evenings.

Recalling my impromptu system for learning Greek, I was resolved now to learn Spanish the same way. The day Bob and I crossed the border at Nuevo Laredo, I told myself with deep concentration, "You're a Mexican." Hours later, having carefully rehearsed my words, I entered a restaurant and asked for something to drink, taking pains to get the accent as correct as I could. An American tourist lady was standing nearby. Hearing me speak, she promptly boosted my confidence by exclaiming in astonishment, "Why, you're a Mexican!"

In one week, by following what was, I realized, a definite principle for self-education, I was speaking Spanish well enough to carry on protracted, if halting, conversations on a wide variety of subjects with people who knew no English. By the end of two and a half months my Spanish was fairly fluent.

The principle, I discovered, is to put oneself completely in tune with whatever subject one wants to master. Inborn talent, though helpful, is not nearly so important as deep concentration. Anyone can do well if he will attune himself sensitively with his subject, and resolutely exclude from his mind any thought of the task's foreignness to him. I have tested this principle many times since then — in learning to write music, to play musical instruments, to paint, to understand some of the deeper aspects of numerous subjects both abstract and practical, to attract money when I needed it, to found a successful community, and to receive helpful answers on countless matters in meditation. Always, the system has taken me far deeper into my subject than intellectual study alone could have done. Friends also, to whom I have taught this principle, have had remarkable success with it.

The principle has many ramifications, one of which is my theory on attracting luck. For a strong, positive affirmation of success is more effective when it is sensitively attuned to one's goal, and protected from the thought of possible failure.

This innocence of the chances of failure is, I think, largely responsible for the phenomenon that is popularly known as "beginners' luck."

An English girl of my acquaintance in Mexico City once told me, "A few weeks ago Mummy and I accompanied Daddy to the racetrack. He goes often, but for us it was the first time. He spent most of the afternoon making fun of our 'system' for betting. We'd choose a horse, you see, because we liked the cute white spot on its nose, or because it had a nice name. Daddy's system was more scientific. But would you believe it? He usually lost, and we won every time!"

If my theory is valid, a beginner's temporary advantage over more seasoned players is that, not knowing the obstacles he is up against, his expectations are more confident. Of course, ignorance of those obstacles also *limits* his success. It takes sensitive awareness of all aspects of a subject, including its difficulties, to achieve genuine mastery.

I had an opportunity during my stay in Mexico to test the mind's power in another way also. Near the end of summer I succumbed to a debilitating combination of diseases: streptococcal infection, tonsillitis, and dysentery. It was several days before I was even strong enough to go see a doctor. When at last I did so, he sent me straight to a hospital. "You'd better reconcile yourself," he told me, "to staying there *at least* two weeks." Worried that I couldn't afford such a long stay, I made a few discreet inquiries, and found that my fears were amply justified. To get money from America would have been difficult, though Dad had left emergency funds there for us boys. The most obvious solution was for me to get well at once.

"You're in perfect health," I told myself firmly, saturating my mind with the thought of well-being, and rigidly excluding from it the slightest indulgence in the thought of my illness. Within two days of my arrival I was out of the hospital, fully cured.

Years later a friend corroborated my belief in the mind's healing power. He had once worked as a physio-therapist in a polio sanitarium. While there, he had noticed that the poor patients, unable to afford a long stay, were more likely to recover than the wealthy ones. He had concluded that their strong desire to get well generated the energy their bodies needed to heal themselves.

My Mexican adventure proved on the whole exciting, interesting, and fun — even though, in its innocent exposure to a wide variety of experiences, it bore some resemblance (as Dad put it later) to the travels of Pinocchio. I didn't get from it, however, what I'd been seeking most keenly: a better way of life. I'd hoped if nothing else to find more laughter there, more human warmth, more inspiration. For a time I imagined I'd actually found them. But then it dawned on me that what I was experiencing was only my own joyous sense of adventure; the people around me, meanwhile, were engrossed in the same dull round of existence as those back home. Mexicans differed only superficially from Americans; in essence both were the same. They lived, worked, bred, and died; the imaginations of a rare few in either land soared above these mundane activities.

Worse still, from my own point of view, I found that I too was basically no different whether in Villa Obregon and Cuernavaca, or in Scarsdale. I experienced the same physical discomforts, the same need to eat and sleep, the same loneliness. I could appreciate more fully now Thoreau's statement with which he dismissed the common fancy that a person was wiser for having traveled abroad. "I have traveled a good deal," he wrote, "in Concord." He had, too. He knew more about his home town and its environs than any other man alive.

The important thing, I realized, is not what we see around us, but the mental attitude with which we look. Answers will not be found merely by transporting one's body from one clime to another. To those people who expect to find abroad what they have overlooked especially *in themselves*, Emerson's words are a classic rebuke: "Travel is a fool's paradise."

In college that fall I was discussing with a few friends a movie we'd seen — *The Razor's Edge*, a tale about a Westerner who traveled to India and, with the help of a wise man whom he met there, found enlightenment.

"Oh, if only I could go to India," cried a girl in our group fervently, *"and get lost!"*

Newly returned as I was from my Mexican experience, I had few illusions left about travel as a solution to the human predicament. "Whom would you lose?" I chuckled. "Certainly not yourself!"

Illness towards the summer's end, and disappointment at not finding what I had hoped to find in Mexico, left me for a time feeling a little dispirited. I continued my search for reality, but with less than my customary enthusiasm. It is a striking fact that, until my faith returned with all its former vitality, Lady Luck withheld from me further proofs of her favor.

Chapter Ten

Intellectual Traps

An Ancient Greek myth says that Icarus and his father, Daedalus, escaped from Crete on artificial wings fashioned by Daedalus out of wax and feathers. Icarus, overconfident with the joy of flying, ignored his father's advice not to soar too high. As he approached nearer and nearer to the sun, the wax on his wings melted, and Icarus plunged to his death in what has been known ever since as the Icarian Sea.

Many of the old Greek myths contain deep psychological and spiritual truths. In this one we find symbolized one of man's all-too-frequent mistakes: In his joy at discovering within himself some hitherto unsuspected power, he "flies too high," ignoring the advice of those who have learned from experience to value humility.

I had discovered that, by will power, faith, and sensitive attunement to certain things that I had wanted to accomplish, I could turn the tide of events to some degree in my favor. I could learn new languages. I could choose to be well, and I was well. I could walk confidently toward certain of life's closed doors, and they opened for me. In all these little successes there had been two key words: *sensitivity* and *attunement*. In learning Greek, I had tried to attune myself sensitively to the Greek consciousness; the important thing had been that attunement, not my mere *resolution* to learn the language. In the affirmation, "I'm a Greek," *Greek*, not *I*, had been the operative word. But now, in my exuberance, I fairly flung myself into the breach. Partly, indeed, I was moved to enthusiasm by the sheer grandeur of my new insights. But because my enthusiasm was excessive, sensitivity and attunement often got lost in the dust cloud kicked up by my overly affirmative ego.

I wanted wisdom. Very well, then: I *was* wise! I wanted my works to inspire and guide people; I wanted to be a great writer. Very well, then: I *was* a great writer! How simple! All I had to do was some fine day produce the poems, plays, and novels that would demonstrate what was already, as far as I was concerned, a *fait accompli*.

The idea probably had a certain merit, but it was marred by the fact that I was reaching too far beyond my own present realities. In the strain involved there was tension; and in the tension, ego.

Faith, if exerted too far beyond a person's actual

capabilities, becomes presumption. Above all it is best always to tie positive affirmations to the whispered guidance of God in the soul. Knowing nothing of such guidance, however, I supplied my own. That which I decreed to be wisdom *was* wisdom. That which I decreed to be greatness *was* greatness. It was not that my opinions were foolish. Many of them were, I believe, fairly sound. But their scope was circumscribed by my own pride. There was no room here for others' opinions. I had not yet learned to listen sensitively to the "truth which comes out of the mouths of babes." Yet I expected ready agreement with my opinions even from those whose age and experience of life gave them some right to consider *me* a babe. I would be no man's disciple. I would blaze my own trails. By vigorous mental affirmation I would bend destiny itself to my will.

Well, I was not the first young man, nor would I be the last, to imagine the popgun in his hand to be a cannon. At least my developing views on life were such that, in time, they refuted my very arrogance.

For my junior year I transferred to Brown University, in Providence, Rhode Island. New perceptions, I felt, would flourish better in a new environment. At Brown I continued my major in English literature, and took additional courses in art appreciation, philosophy, and geology. But my attitude toward formal education was growing increasingly cavalier. I didn't see of what possible use a degree would be to me in my chosen career as a writer. Nor did I have much patience with an accumulation of mere facts, when it was the *why* of things I was after. Even our philosophy course, which ought to have been at least relatively concerned with the *whys*, was devoted to categorizing the mere *opinions* of the men we were studying. When I found I wasn't expected to concern myself with the *validity* of their opinions, I took to reading poetry in the classsroom in silent protest.

Intent on developing the identity I had selected for myself, I played the role, for all who cared to listen to me, of established author and philosopher. A few people actually did listen. For hours they and I sat together, engrossed in the adventure of philosophical thought. I got them to see that joy *has* to be the real purpose of life, that nonattachment is the surest key to joy, and that one ought to live simply, seeking joy not in things, but in an ever-expanding vision of reality. Truth can be found, I insisted, not in the sordid aspects of life, as so many writers claim, but in the heights of human aspiration.

Most of the writing of my student days has long since been consigned to fire and blessed oblivion. One piece, however, which escaped the holocaust expresses some of the views I was expounding at that time. It may serve a useful purpose for me to quote it here, unedited.

"My countrymen, having begotten what is in many respects a monstrosity, go about saying what had never before been said so strongly, that we must go with the age if we would create great things. That it is necessary for them to repeat what should normally be too obvious for repetition, shows how slight is the hold this century has on our hearts.

"They have, moreover, misunderstood the true meaning of democracy, which is not (as they suppose) to debase the noble man while singing the virtues of the common man, but rather to tell the common man that he, too, can now become noble. The object of democracy is to raise the lowly, and not to praise them for being low. It is only with such a goal that it can have any real merit.

"God's law is right and beautiful. No ugliness exists except man's injustice and the symbols of it. It is not life in the raw we see when we pass through the slums, not the naked truth that many 'realists' would have us see, but the facts and figures of our injustice, the distortion of life and the corruption of truth. If we would claim to be realistic it is not reality we shall see from the squalid depths of humanity, for our view will be premised on injustice and negation. Goodness and beauty will appear bizarre, whereas misery, hatred and all the sad children of man's misunderstanding will seem normal, and yet strange withal and unfounded, as if one could see the separate leaves and branches of a tree and yet could find no trunk. It is not from the hovel of a pauper that we can see all truth, but from the dwelling place of a saint; for from his mountain, ugliness itself is seen, not as darkness, but as lack of light, and the squalor of cities will be no longer foreign, but a native wrong, understood at the core as a symptom of our own injustice.

"The more closely we watch the outside as a means to understand from the inside, the farther off the inside withdraws from our understanding. The same with people as with God."

My ideas were, I think, basically valid. But ideas alone do not constitute wisdom. Truth must be lived. I'm afraid that, in endless discussions about truth, the sweet taste of it still eluded me.

One day a friend and I were crossing campus on our way back from a class. Lovingly he turned to me and remarked, "If ever I've met a genius in my life, it is you."

For a moment I felt flattered. But as I reflected on his words, shame swept over me like a wave. What had I actually done to deserve his praise? I had *talked*! I had been so busy talking that I hadn't even had much time left over for writing. And his compliment had been so sincere! It was one thing to have played the part of the author and philosopher to convince *myself*. It was quite another that my acting had convinced others. I felt like a hypocrite. Sick with self-disappointment, I withdrew from then on from most of my associates at Brown, and sought to express in literature the truths I had hitherto been treating so lightly as coffee shop conversation.

It didn't take me very long to realize that it is much easier to talk hit-or-miss philosophy over a coffee table than to transform basic concepts into meaningful writing. There are levels of understanding that come only when one has lived a truth deeply over a space of years. Initial insights may suggest almost the same words, yet the power of those words will be as nothing compared to the conviction ringing in them when their truths have been deeply lived.

St. Anthony, in the early part of the Christian era, was called from his desert hermitage by the bishop of Alexandria to speak in defense of the divinity of Jesus Christ. Arguments had been raging throughout Christendom as a result of the so-called Arian heresy, which denied Christ's oneness with God. St. Anthony gave no long, carefully reasoned homily in defense of his ideas. His words, however, charged as they were with the fervor of a lifetime of prayer and meditation, conveyed such a depth of power that, among his listeners, further argument ceased. All St. Anthony said was, "I have *seen* Him!"

Alas, I had *not* seen Him. Nor had I deeply lived a single truth. My painting was more a sketch than a finished work. Try as I would to express my ideas in writing, the moment I picked up a pen I found my mind growing strangely vague. Whatever I did write was more to develop my literary technique than to express what I really wanted to say. I described situations with which I wasn't familiar. I wrote about people whose living counterparts I had never met. To master my craft, I imitated the styles of others, hoping to find in their phrasing and choice of words secrets to clarity and beauty of self-expression that I might develop later into a style of my own.

I had the satisfaction of being praised by certain professors and professional men of letters. Some of them told me I would someday become a front-ranking writer. But at nineteen I was far from justifying their friendly expectations. Worst of all, in my own opinion, was the fact that I was saying almost nothing really worthwhile.

I worked on the psychological effects, in poetry, of different patterns of rhyme and rhythm. I studied the emotion-charged rhythms of Irish-English, which the great Irish playwright, John Millington Synge, captured so beautifully. I wondered why modern English, by comparison, was so barren of deep feeling, and pondered how, without sounding studied and unnatural, to bring beauty to dramatic speech.

One of the dogmas I had been taught in English classes was that iambic pentameter, the blank verse form of Shakespearean drama, is the most natural poetic rhythm for speech in the English language. Shakespeare, of course, was trotted out as the ultimate proof of this dogma. But in *modern* English, blank verse sounded to me much too courtly. Maxwell Anderson, the Twentieth-Century American playwright, used it in several of his plays, and the best I could say of them was that they were brave attempts. I certainly didn't want to confine myself to the sterile formulae modern writers so often follow who try to render speech realistically. ("Ya wanna come?" "Yeah, yeah, *sure*." "Hey look, I'm not beggin' ya. Just take it or leave it." "Okay, okay, smart boy. Who says I don't wanna come?") Shakespeare, even when imitating common speech, idealized it. My problem was how to follow his example without sounding artificial. If literary language couldn't uplift, there seemed little point in calling it literature.

For summer vacation in 1946 I went to Provincetown, on Cape Cod — a haven for artists and writers. There I rented a small room, turned an upsidedown dresser drawer into a desk, and devoted myself to writing a one-act play. To make the few dollars I had stretch as far as possible, I ate the chef's special at a local diner for lunch every day. For forty-five cents I got a greasy beef stew with one or two soggy slices of potato in it, and, if I was lucky, two or three slices of carrot. After two months of this daily banquet, even the bargain price could no longer tempt me to endure such punishment another day. I went into the diner one afternoon, ordered the chef's special, watched a slice of potato disintegrate as I stabbed it half-heartedly with a spoon, then got up and walked out again, never to return.

Toward the end of the summer I spent a week on a distant beach, "far from the madding crowd." (How wonderful it would be, I thought, to be a real hermit!) My one-act play, which I finished on those dunes, didn't turn out badly, though I hadn't been able to shake off the hypnotic charm of Synge's English.

The summer itself was pleasant also, despite my penury. But above all what it did was show me that I was as much an outsider in artistic circles as in any other. Increasingly it was becoming clear that I would never find what I was seeking by *becoming* anything. To say, "I'm a writer," or even, "I'm a great writer," wasn't at all the answer. What I needed above all concerned the deeper question of *what I was already.*

Chapter Eleven

By-Paths

LIVING IN PROVIDENCE, a short train ride away from Boston, I often visited Rod and Betty. Rod lived in Wellesley Hills, a Boston suburb. Betty, a dear friend as well as my cousin, was a student at nearby Wellesley College.

Rod had enrolled at Boston University. He was as good-humored and intense about everything as ever. Together we devoted much time to what might, with some generosity, be described as the Indian practice of *neti, neti* ("not this, not that").*
That is to say, we engaged in a running analysis, complete with droll commentary and merry exaggeration, on some of the follies to which mankind is

---

*By examining every human delusion dispassionately, abandoning each with the conclusion, "This, too, is unreal (*neti, neti*)," the seeker arrives at last at the vision of perfect Truth.

addicted.

There was the living-to-impress-others dream: "I work on Wall Street. (*Pause*) Of course, you know what *that* means."

There was the "Protestant ethic," I'm-glad-I'm-not-happy-because-that-means-I'm-good dream: "I wouldn't *think* of telling you what you ought to do. All I ask is that you (*sigh*) let your conscience be your guide."

A favorite of ours was the if-you-want-to-be-sure-you're-right-just-follow-the-crowd dream: "You'd better march in step, son, if you want the whole column to move."

Rod was a wonderful mimic. He could make even normally reasonable statements sound ridiculous. He attained his height when imitating someone hopelessly inept trying to sound like a big shot.

We also discussed seriously the fulfillments we both wanted from life. The longer we talked, the longer our list of minuses kept growing, and the shorter that of the plusses. For Rod, these narrowing horizons meant his gradual loss of ambition to become a writer. For me, it meant a gradual redirection of ambition from worldly to divine attainments.

In those days, as I've mentioned earlier, students were not as preoccupied as they are nowadays with the search for meaning. For most of them the ideal was, "Get to the top; become wealthy and important; marry; buy a big home, and populate it with a large family; let everyone see you enjoying life; better still, get them to *envy* you for enjoying it." Needless to say, the gradations of worldly ambition are many, by no means all of them crass. But youth in its quest for personal directions is seldom sensitive to the directions of others. If Rod and I were ungenerous, it was partly because we were still preoccupied with defining our own goals.

Not surprisingly, some of the people whose values we rejected reciprocated with a certain antagonism. Rod, in fact, almost invited their antagonism, by judging *them* along with their values. Ever tending to extremes in his reactions, he either praised people to the skies as "perfectly wonderful," or condemned them to the depths as "dreadful," or "ridiculous."

But judgment forms a barrier: In excluding others, it also encloses oneself. Rod, by his judgmental attitude, was gradually painting himself into a psychological corner. After all, if others didn't measure up to his ideals, it behooved him to prove that *he* did. The stricter his standards for others, the more impossible they became for himself. I remember a space of two or three months when, though supposedly working on a novel, he never progressed beyond typing, "Page one, Chapter one," on an otherwise blank page. In time I suppose he had no choice but to abandon writing altogether. It was a pity, for his was, and still is, one of the most talented, intelligent, and deeply perceptive natures I have ever known.

I myself, though not as judgmental as Rod, could be cutting in my remarks. I justified this tendency by telling myself that I was only trying to get people to be more discriminating. But there is never a *good* excuse for unkindness. In one important respect, indeed, my fault was greater than Rod's, for whereas his judgments were directed at people he scarcely knew, my criticisms were reserved for my friends.

I once wrote a stinging letter to Betty, simply because I felt that she wasn't trying hard enough to develop her own very real spiritual potential. Occasionally even my mother came under fire from me. It was years, and many personal hurts, before I realized that no one has a right to impose on the free will of another human being. Respect for that freedom is, indeed, essential if one would counsel others wisely. Without due regard for another's right to be himself, one's perception of his needs will be insensitive, and seldom wholly accurate. I, certainly, had all the insensitivity of immature understanding. The hurts I gave others were never compensated for by any notable acceptance, on their part, of my advice.

Often on the path I have thought, How can I make amends for the hurts I have given so many of my friends and loved ones? And as often the answer comes back to me: By asking God to bless them with *His* love.

Towards the end of my first year at Brown, Rod, having dropped out of Boston University, came to live with me in a room I had taken off campus. We cooked our own meals with the help of a book that I had bought for its reassuring title, *You Can Cook if You Can Read*. I'd always looked on cooking as a kind of magic. It delighted me, therefore, to find in this book such quasi-ritualistic advice as, "To ascertain if the spaghetti is done, throw a piece of it at a wall. If it sticks there, it's ready to eat."

Rooming with Rod, I got an opportunity to observe on a new level the truth, which I'd discovered during my last semester at Haverford, that subjective attitudes can have objective consequences. Rod's tendency to judge others attracted antagonism not only from people he knew, but, in some subtle way, from perfect strangers. In restaurants, people sitting nearby would sometimes snarl at him for no evident reason. One evening a passer-by pulled a gun on him, warning him to mind his own business. Another evening six men with knives chased him down a dark street; Rod eluded them only by hiding in a doorway. Whenever he and I went out together, all was peaceful. But Rod by himself continually skirted disaster. Fortunately, no doubt because he really meant no harm, he always got off without injury.

At this time Rod's life and mine were beginning to branch apart. Rod shared some of my interest in spiritual matters, but not to the extent of wanting to get involved in them himself. I, on the other hand, was growing more and more keen to mold my life along spiritual lines. We talked freely on most subjects, but on this one I found it better to keep my thoughts to myself.

One day I was reading a book, when suddenly I had an inspiration that came, I felt, from some deeper-than-conscious level of my mind. Stunned at the depth of my certitude, I told Rod, "I'm going to be a religious teacher!"

"Don't be silly!" he snorted, not at all impressed. *Very well*, I thought, *I'll say no more. But I know.*

The Search

The thought of being a religious teacher, however, in no way inspired me to spend more time in church, where religion held no appeal for me whatever. "Hel-*lo*!" our campus minister would simper sweetly, almost embarrassingly self-conscious in his effort to demonstrate his "Christian charity" to us when passing us in the hallway. People, I thought, attended church chiefly because it was the respectable and proper thing to do. Some of them, no doubt, wanted to be good, but how many, I wondered, attended because they *loved God*? Divine yearning seemed incompatible, somehow, with going to church, carefully ordered as the services were, and devoid of spontaneity. The ministers in their pulpits talked of politics and sin and social ills — and, endlessly, of money. But they didn't talk of God. They didn't tell us to dedicate our lives to Him. No hint passed their lips that the soul's only true Friend and Lover dwells within, a truth which Jesus stated plainly. Socially inconvenient Biblical teachings, such as Jesus' commandment, "*Leave all*, and follow me," were either omitted altogether from their homilies, or hemmed in with cautious qualifications that left us, in the end, exactly where we were already, armed now with a good excuse. My impression was that the ministers I listened to hesitated to offend their wealthy parishioners, whom they viewed as customers. As for direct, *inner* communion with God, no one ever mentioned it. Communion was something one took at the altar rail, with priestly assistance.

One Sunday I attended a service in a little town north of Boston. The sermon title was, "Drink to

Forget." And what were we supposed to forget? Well, the wicked Japs and their betrayal of us at Pearl Harbor. The Nazis and their atrocities. There was nothing here about righting our own wrongs, or seeing God in our enemies. Nothing even about forgiving them *their* wrongs. The sacrificial wine that was served later that morning was supposed to help us forget all the bad things *others* had done to us. I could hardly suppress a smile when that Lethe-inducing nectar turned out to be, not wine, but grape juice!

If there was one subject that roused me to actual bitterness, it was the utterly commonplace character of religion as I found it in the churches. My bitterness was not because the demands this religion made were impossible, but because they were so unspeakably trivial; not because its assertions were unbelievable, but because they were carefully maintained at the safest, most timid level of popular acceptability. Above all I was disturbed because the churches struck me as primarily social institutions, not as lighthouses to guide people out of the darkness of spiritual ignorance. It was almost as if they were trying to *reconcile* themselves to that ignorance. With dances, third-class entertainments, and diluted teachings they tried desperately to get people merely to come to church, while neglecting the commandment of Jesus, "Feed my sheep." Frank Laubach, the great Christian missionary, once launched a campaign to get more ministers simply to *mention* God in their sermons. His campaign suggests the deepest reason for my own disillusionment. Of all things in life, it was for spiritual understanding that I longed most urgently. Yet, most notably, it was the churches that withheld such understanding from me. Instead, they offered me dead substitutes. For years I sought through other channels the fulfillment I craved, because the ministers in their pulpits made a mockery of the very fulfillments promised in the Bible. To paraphrase the words of Jesus, I asked of them the bread of life, and they offered me a stone.*

Thus, hungry as I was for spiritual understanding, I saw no choice but to pursue my career as a writer, and looked to the arts for that kind of inspiration which, had I but known it, only God can supply. It was like walking into a void, for lack of any better place to go. An emptiness was growing in my heart, and I knew not how to fill it.

My college classes were becoming increasingly burdensome. Intellectualism was not bringing me wisdom. It seemed to me almost unbearably trivial to be studying the Eighteenth-Century novel, when it was the meaning of life itself I was trying to fathom.

My parents had recently returned from Rumania. I sought their permission to take a leave of absence from college. Reluctantly they gave it. Thus, midway through my senior year, I left Brown University, never to return.

Thereafter for several months I lived with my parents. I struggled — gamely, perhaps, but without real hope — over a two-act play. It concerned nothing I really wanted to say. But then, the things I did want to say were the last I felt myself decently

*Matthew 7:9.

qualified to express.

Occasionally I went into New York City, and spent hours there walking about, gazing at the tragedy of worldly people's transition from loneliness to apathy. How bereft of joy they seemed, struggling for mere survival in those desolate canyons of concrete!

At other times I would stroll through the happier setting of Washington Square, almost in a kind of ecstasy, observing mothers with their babies, laughing children playing on the lawns, young people singing with guitars by the fountain, trees waving, the fountain spray playing colorfully in the sunlight. All seemed to be joined together in a kind of cosmic symphony, their many lives but one life, their countless ripples of laughter but one sea of joy.

The valleys and the peaks of life! What grand truth could bind them all together, making them one?

Back home one day I told Mother I wouldn't be going with her to church any more. This was one of the few times I have ever seen her weep. "It pains me so deeply," she cried, "to see you pulling away from God!" I wasn't aware of her promise, made before my birth, to give me, her first-born, to God. I would have loved in any case to reassure her, and was deeply touched by her concern for me. But what could I do? My duty above all was to be honest with myself.

A few days later Mother sought me out. Hopefully she quoted a statement that she had read somewhere that morning, to the effect that atheism sometimes presages a deep spiritual commitment. I

The Search

was by no means the atheist she thought I was; nevertheless, it relieved me to see that she understood my rejection of her church as part, at least, of a sincere search for truth. I didn't explain my true feelings to her at the time, however, for fear of diluting the intensity of my search.

That summer I traveled up to the little town of Putney, Vermont, where my youngest brother Dick was in school. Dick was maturing into a fine young man; I loved him deeply. Something he'd told me had touched me particularly. One day he was driving to a house to pick up a group of friends. As his car was rolling slowly to a halt, it lightly touched a dog that was standing complacently before it. The dog wasn't hurt, but its owner, a small, older man, no physical match for Dick, was furious. Striding up to the car, he punched Dick in the jaw.

At that moment Dick's friends came out of the house. Dick, concerned that they might hurt the man if they knew what had happened, said nothing of the matter either to them or to him.

During my stay at Putney, a drama teacher there recommended the Dock Street theater in Charleston, South Carolina, as a good place to study stagecraft. For my twenty-first birthday Dad had given me five hundred dollars. (Dick's comment: "A pleasing precedent has been set!") I decided, albeit in rather a mood of desperation, that if I was going to be a playwright I might as well go to Charleston with this money, and gain direct experience in my craft at that theater.

Chapter Twelve

"Who Am I? What Is God?"

"ALL THE WORLD'S A STAGE," Jaques says in *As You Like It*.

Few people realize how little their personalities represent them as they really are. Emerson wrote, in "The Over-Soul," "We know better than we do. We do not yet possess ourselves, and we know at the same time that we are much more. I feel the same truth how often in my trivial conversation with my neighbors, that somewhat higher in each of us overlooks this by-play, and Jove nods to Jove from behind each of us. Men descend to meet."

Every man in his soul is divine. He merely persuades himself, by concentration on his outer life, that he is a baker, banker, teacher, or preacher; that he is rude or sensitive, athletic or lazy, genial or solemn. He sees not that all these are but roles, reflections of the likes and dislikes, the desires and aversions that he has accumulated over incarnations. What has once been acquired can as surely once again be shed. The outer self changes endlessly. Only in his inner Self is man changeless and eternal.

Much of my life seems, in retrospect, almost as though it had been planned for me. Certainly my experiences up to this time in my narrative reflect, basically, the lessons I needed to learn. It was perhaps due to this same "suspicious Someone's" plan for me that I spent the better part of the next year working with the Dock Street Theater, in Charleston. The various roles I acted, quite unprofessionally, on its stage, taught me to stand back from myself mentally, to observe this peculiar specimen, Donald Walters, acting out his normal daily role as a young American male of somewhat cheerful disposition, an aspiring playwright, and a more or less perennial innocent abroad.

My associations at the Dock Street Theater helped me, in time, to see the shallowness of *all* role-playing, whether in or out of the theater. For most of the people I met there were always "on stage"; they based their very self-esteem on how well they could pretend. A year spent with them added immeasurably to my yearning for values that were *true*.

I arrived in Charleston toward the end of June. The Dock Street Theater, I learned, had closed for the summer months, and was not scheduled to open again until September. I took a room in a small boarding house where I received lodging and three generous meals a day for only ten dollars a week.

The atmosphere was pleasantly familial. Most of my fellow boarders were students at The Citadel, a nearby college for men. The friendship of congenial companions my own age threatened for a time my intentions of devoting myself to writing. Rationalizing the threat, I told myself that, as a budding writer, I needed to absorb all I could of local color. Aside from a few scattered poems, my "accomplishments" now were limited to a succession of parties, outings to the beach, and merry bull sessions where everything was discussed from politics to girls to local gossip.

Gradually I expanded my frontiers to a study of the way people lived on various levels of Charleston society. I went everywhere; met people in every walk of life, explored some of the dingiest "dives," and was a guest in several prominent homes.

Charleston was a small city of some 70,000 people. I found it possible to discover within its narrow boundaries a representative cross section of America. With the middle and upper social strata, and to a lesser degree with the lower, I was already somewhat familiar. But those lower strata which I now encountered were an eye-opener. I'm referring not to the poor, whose simple dignity often gives the like to that condescending designation, "lower class," but to people, some of them actually wealthy, whose meanness of heart and narrow outlook condemned them to lives of criminal greed. Included among this type were the owners and operators of sordid speak-easies, which posed as fronts for still-more-illicit gambling rooms upstairs, and (one suspected) for other hush-hush activities as well. These people projected an almost visible aura of dishonesty, of cold brutality and evil. Some of them, as I say, were wealthy, but their riches had been acquired from feeding on human desperation.

Equally sordid were the lives of most of the people who frequented these places. For the customers, too, were out purely for what they could get for themselves. Their conversation reflected a hardness; their brittle laughter crackled like ice. Such people were the perennially homeless — in consciousness, if not in fact. They were men and women who wandered aimlessly from city to city, seeking transient jobs and still more transient pleasures; individuals whose character was fast losing distinction in the blur of alcoholic fumes; couples whose family lives were disintegrating under jackhammer blows of incessant bickering; lonely people who hoped blindly to find in this wilderness of human indifference just a glimpse of friendship.

Everywhere I saw desolation. This, I reflected, was the stuff of which countless plays and novels had been written. *Why* this preoccupation with negativity? Is great literature something merely to be endured? Who can possibly gain anything worthwhile from exposure to sterility and hopelessness?

Yet these, undeniably, were a part of life too. Their effect on me spiritually, moreover, proved to some extent wholesome. For the awareness they gave me of man's potential for self-degradation lent urgency to my own longing to explore a higher potential.

I took another stab, consequently, at attending church. I even enrolled in a church choir. But soon I discovered that this was only exchanging one kind of sterility for another. The church atmosphere was more wholesome, no doubt, but partly for that very reason it was also more smug, more resistant to any suggestion that some higher perfection might be attainable.

Civilized man prides himself on how far advanced his present state is beyond that of the primitive savage. He looks condescendingly on tribal cultures for their practice of endowing trees, wind, rain, and heavenly bodies with human personalities. Now that science has explained everything in prosaic terms, modern man considers himself wiser for the loss of his sense of awe. But I'm not so sure that he deserves congratulation. It strikes me rather that, dazzled by his own technology, he has only developed a new sort of superstition, one infinitely less interesting. Too pragmatic now to worship, he has forgotten how to commune. Instead of relating sensitively to the universe around him, he shuts it out of his life with concrete "jungles," air conditioning, and "muzak"; with self-promotion and noisy entertainments; and with an obsession with problems that are real for him only because he *gives* them reality. He is like a violin string without a sounding board. Life, when cut off from broader realities, becomes thin and meaningless.

Modern technology alienates us from the universe, and from one another. Worst of all, it alienates us from ourselves. It directs all our energies toward the mere manipulation of *things*, until we ourselves assume almost thing-like qualities. In how many modern plays and novels are men idealized for their ability to act with the precision, emotionlessness, and efficiency of a machine. We are taught to behave in this world like rude guests, gracelessly consuming our host's offerings without offering him a single word of thanks in return. Such is our approach to nature, to God, to life itself. We make ourselves petty, then imagine the universe petty also. We rob our own lives of meaning, then call life as a whole meaningless. Smug in our unknowing, we make a dogma of ignorance. And when, in this "civilized" smugness of ours, we approach the question of religion, we address God Himself as though he had better watch His manners if He would be worthy of a place on our altars.

After a month or so of paddling in the waters of Charleston's social life, I finally decided that I'd exposed myself quite enough to cross sections of a society whose members seemed at least as ignorant as I was. None of my new acquaintances had contributed anything positive to my search for meaning. And of "local color," I felt that I had seen altogether too many browns and greys.

My own "purism," of course, held a certain smugness of its own. Had I been less rigidly critical in my attitudes, I might have attracted more uplifting human associations. Or I might have discovered in the very people I was meeting qualities truer than I dreamed. On the other hand, to do myself justice, it was to a great extent with the very aim of overcoming such rigidity in my own nature that I had made it a practice to mix with so many different types of people.

Toward the end of the summer I moved out of

my boarding house to a small apartment at 60 Tradd Street. Here I began writing a one-act comedy titled, *Religion in the Park*. Bitter as well as funny, the play concerned a woman who wanted to live a religious life, and who eagerly sought instruction from a priest, only to have him discourage her every devotional sentiment with his careful emphasis on religious propriety. Meanwhile a passing tramp rekindled her fervor with tales of a saint who, he claimed, had cured him of lameness. Here at last was what she'd been seeking: religion *lived*, religion *experienced*, not couched in mere social customs and theoretical dogmas!

But, alas, in the end the tramp proved a fraud. An alcoholic, he had merely invented his tale in the hope of coaxing a few easy dollars into his pocket.

This woman's hope and subsequent disillusionment reflected my own spiritual longings, and the skepticism that continued to prevent my actual commitment to the religious life.

An interesting sidelight on that one-act play is that the "saint," according to the tramp's story, lived in California — the very state where I was later to meet my guru. Could I have been aware, on some deep level of my consciousness, that that was where my own destiny lay? Once as a child, while crossing the Atlantic, I had met a boy from California. I remember thinking as I heard the name, "*That* is where I must go someday." Years later, when first contemplating that trip to Mexico, I had considered briefly whether I might go to California instead. Then I had put aside the idea with the verdict, "It isn't yet time." Emerson's words come back to me now, more in question than in certainty: "We know better than we do." *Had* I known?

When the Dock Street Theater opened in September, I went there to seek affiliation with it, but was told that the only way I could do so officially was to enroll as a student in its drama school. Counting myself well out of the academic scene, I asked if I might not be given some other status. Finally the director permitted me, partly on the strength of my new play, to affiliate with them as an "unofficial" student. Under this arrangement I was able to study stagecraft in the evenings, and at the same time to devote my days to writing.

During the following months I acted in a variety of plays, mingled freely with teachers and official students, and served in a number of useful, if more or less nondescript, capacities. These activities gave me some understanding of the business of staging plays, particularly in a small community theater. As an actor, however, I'm afraid I was something of a disaster. "This isn't *me!*" I kept thinking. "How will I ever learn who I really am, if I keep on playing people I'm not?" From a standpoint of my intended profession as a playwright, however, the experience was worthwhile.

The daylight hours I spent by myself, at first writing, and then, increasingly, thinking, thinking over my old problems: What is the purpose of life? Who am I? Hasn't man a destiny higher than (I looked about me in desperation) — than *this*? Most important of all, what is true happiness? How can it be found?

During the time that I spent writing, I threw

myself into the task of developing the techniques of my craft. Curiously perhaps, for a budding playwright, I wrote no plays at this time; I wanted to keep my mind flexible to pursue new directions in stagecraft as they presented themselves in the theater. Instead I wrote poetry, and sought — still — to develop a sense for poetic speech in drama. I also pondered the theater's potential for inspiring a far-reaching spiritual renaissance. To this end I studied the plays of the Spanish playwright, Federico Garcia Lorca, to see whether his surrealistic style might be adapted to induce in people a more mystical awareness.

My probing thoughts, however, led one by one to a dead end. How much, after all, can the theater really accomplish? Did even Shakespeare, great as he was, effect any deep-seated changes in the lives of man? None, surely, at any rate, compared with those which religion has inspired. I shuddered at this comparison, for I loved Shakespeare, and found little to attract me in the churches. But the conclusion, whether I liked it or not, was inescapable: Religion, for all its fashionable mediocrity, its sham, its devotion to the things of this world, remains the most powerfully beneficial influence on earth. Not art, not music, not literature, not science, politics, conquest, or technology: The only truly uplifting power in history, always, has been religion.

How was this possible? Puzzled, I decided to probe beneath the surface, to discover what deep-seated element religion contained that was vital and true.

Avoiding what I considered the trap of institutionalized religion, of "churchianity," I took to walking or sitting for hours on end by the ocean, pondering its immensity. I watched little fingers of water rushing in among the rocks and pebbles on the shore. Did the vastness of God find *personal* expression, similarly, in our own lives?

The juxtaposition of these thoughts with my daily contacts in and out of the theater filled me with distaste. How petty seemed man's desires compared to the impersonal vastness of infinity! The loftiest aspirations of most of the people around me seemed mean, their values to an incredible degree selfish and ignoble. Egos pitted themselves against other egos in childish rivalries. My fellow students insisted that such behavior laid bare the realities of human nature: So, in fact, had declared the modern dramas they admired, and, far from bemoaning these "realities," they gloried in them. Aspiring actors that they were, they prided themselves on pretending selfishness, "rugged egoism," indifference to the needs of others, and rudeness — until the pretence itself became their reality.

My associates of those days helped me spiritually more than I was capable of realizing at the time. The more they mocked me with their insistent claim, "This is life!" the more my heart cried, "It isn't! It *can't* be!" And as the urgency of my cry deepened me in my own search, I grew to understand that what they termed *life* was nothing but living death.

This isn't to say, however, that sordidness has no objective reality. God was trying to get me to see, rather, the depths to which man can sink, without Him.

"Who Am I? What Is God?"

One evening outside my apartment I met a fellow student walking in a daze, scarcely able to tread a straight line. At first I thought he must be drunk, but then I noticed dried blood on his forehead. Evidently there was something more serious amiss. I led him indoors. Between long pauses of mental confusion, he related the following story:

"I was sitting quietly on a park bench, enjoying the evening air. I remember hearing footsteps approaching behind me. The next thing I knew I was lying on the grass, slowly returning to consciousness. My coat and trousers were gone. So was my wallet.

"Minutes passed. Dazed as I was, I had no idea what to do. Then I saw a police car parked on the far side of the park. Relieved, I staggered over to it and explained my predicament. Naturally, I assumed they'd want to help me.

"Well, can you guess what they did? They arrested me for being indecently dressed! At the police station I was put into a jail cell without so much as a chance to protest.

"For some time I tried to get them at least to let me make a phone call. Finally they made that much of a concession. 'Just one call,' the sergeant said. I phoned a couple of friends of ours, who came over with fresh clothing.

"Now — would you believe it? — *our friends* are in jail, and *I'm* out!" Shaking his head incredulously, "I still don't understand how it all happened."

What had happened, I learned later, was that these friends, infuriated at the policemen's indifference, had cried, "You don't even seem to care that a crime has been committed!"

"You're under arrest!" bellowed the police sergeant.

Our friends resisted this further outrage, and were set upon by all the policemen in the room, beaten up, and thrown into jail. My injured friend, meanwhile, was released, presumably because he was decently dressed now, and told to go home and forget the whole thing. It was hardly fifteen minutes later that I met him wandering about, dazed and confused.

I returned with him immediately to the police station. As we entered, wild screams were issuing from a back room. Moments later a couple of policemen emerged, dragging a screaming black woman across the floor by her heels. They dumped her unceremoniously in front of the sergeant's desk, where she passed out. One of the men, evidently considering her silence disrespectful, fetched a rubber hose and beat her with it on the soles of her bare feet until she regained consciousness and started screaming again. Satisfied, they dragged her into the jail and flung her, still screaming, into a cell. The remainder of the time we were there I heard her moaning quietly.

Throughout this grim episode the rest of the policemen in the room, about fifteen of them, stood about, laughing. "I haven't had this much fun in *years*!" gloated one of them, rubbing his hands together.

Obviously, to reason with such brutes was impossible; I therefore tried getting information out of them. The sergeant finally gave me the name of some judge whose word he required, he said, "Before I can release those hoodlums." It was already late, but before the night ended I succeeded in getting the judge out of bed, and our friends out of jail.

From this utter mockery of justice I at least learned a salutary lesson. First, of course, I reacted with normal, human indignation at such brutality. But subsequent reflection convinced me that injustice of one kind or another is inevitable in this world. For aren't all of us to some extent lost in ignorance? Blind as I myself was, what right had I to blame others, simply because their blindness differed from my own? My first thought had been, "We need a revolution!" But then I realized that what was needed was a new kind of revolution: religious, not social.

Religion. Again that word! This time I was being pushed toward it by human injustice instead of pulled by my own longing for some higher good. I began now to wonder if evil weren't a conscious will in the universe. How else to account for its prevalence on earth? for the cruelty of man to man? the brutality of the Nazis? the terrors that millions suffer under communism? How else to explain the appalling twist of fate that causes the good intentions of many who embrace communism to result in human debasement, slavery, and death? What, outside of a renewed, widespread return to God — *a spiritual revolution* — could correct the almost unimaginable wrongs in this world?

I gave much thought at this time to communism as a force for evil. My parents had returned from Rumania with tales of Russian atrocities. Our Rumanian friends there were suffering under the new regime; some of them had been deported to slave labor camps in Russia. Surely, I thought, the common argument against communism, that it is inefficient, misses the point altogether. What is truly wrong with it is not that its top-heavy bureaucracy results in the production of fewer material conveniences, nor even that it denies men their political rights, but that it treats materialism* itself as a virtual religion. Denying the reality of God, it sets up matter in His place, and demands self-abnegation of its adherents much as religions do everywhere. For committed communists, the shortage of material goods reveals, not the inefficiency of their system, but the measure of their willingness to sacrifice for "the cause." Believing in nothing higher than matter, they see spiritual values — truthfulness, compassion, love — as utterly meaningless. They feel morally justified, rather, in committing any atrocity, as long as it advances their own ideological ends. Their motto is, "In every circumstance, think only what is best for the cause."

Theirs might be called a religion of unconsciousness, of non-values. It does offer, however, a pseudo-moralistic rationale for the materialistic values of our age. For this reason, I'm afraid, its teachings will continue to spread, until men everywhere embrace another, truer kind of religion, one that places God, not matter, at the center of reality.

Pursuing these thoughts, I found myself for both objective and subjective reasons, for the sake of

---

*Materialism, in this context, refers to the philosophical theory that all phenomena, including those of the mind, must be attributed to material agencies.

mankind generally as well as for my own personal development, drawn to the conclusion that what I wanted, what all men really needed, was God.

With ever more pressing urgency the question returned to me: *What IS God?*

One evening, taking a long walk into the gathering night, I deeply pondered this problem. I dismissed at the outset the popular notion that a venerable figure with flowing white beard, piercing eyes, and a terrible brow presides over the universe, with its billions of galaxies. But, I thought, what about the abstract alternatives that more thoughtful people have suggested — vague definitions such as "Cosmic Ground of Being," which leave one with little to do but close the book and see what is playing on the radio? No, I thought, the God I was seeking must be a *dynamic force*, one that could transform my life, else there was no point in seeking Him.

Well, then, I continued, if He *was* a force, might He possibly be a blind force, sort of like electricity? I'd heard Him so described. There would, of course, be little point in calling such a force, God. But in any case, the argument didn't hold together. For if God was blind, whence sprang human intelligence?

Materialists I knew claimed that everything, including intelligence, evolved quite accidentally out of random combinations of electrons. According to them, the universe isn't marvelous at all. It only *seems* marvelous to us because, in the long struggle for survival, man happened to evolve a capacity for wonder as one of the conditioned responses of his emotional mechanism. But this proposition I had long discarded as absurd.

We all know the signs of exceptional intelligence in man: the bright, alert expression in the eyes, the prompt responses, the general air of competence. An intelligent person may pretend successfully to be stupid, but a stupid person can never successfully pretend to be intelligent. What then of the universe, revealing as it does so many signs of an extraordinary intelligence? The intricate organization of stars, atoms, and creatures, the amazingly exact laws on which the cosmos operates — could a mindless force have created these? Impossible! Only egotists, surely, in their desire to claim the highest intelligence for themselves and their kind, could overlook the evidence all around them of an intelligence far mightier than their own.

Continuing this line of reasoning, I thought, if the wonders of creation are the outward signs of a conscious, intelligent Creator, then surely one of the most wonderful of such signs is intelligence itself. Indeed, if human and animal consciousness manifest the *principle* of intelligence, and if God, as universal Intelligence, *is* that principle, then human intelligence is a manifestation, however imperfect, of God!

Suddenly I felt I was very near to solving my problem. For surely, I reasoned, if God's intelligence is manifested through man, then the Lord cannot exist wholly outside His creation — like some heavenly traffic cop, I thought wryly, from a distance directing human lives here below. If to any degree we, in our intelligence, manifest His infinite intelligence, this can only mean that *we are a part of Him*.

What a staggering concept!

A further thought came: If our lives and consciousness are His manifestations, might it not be possible for us, by deepening our awareness of Him, *to manifest Him more perfectly*?

I recalled the days I had spent watching the ocean surf breaking into long, restless fingers among the rocks and pebbles on the shore. The width of each opening, I reflected, determined the size of the water's flow. Similarly, if the deepest reality of our lives is God, might it not be possible for us to chip away at the granite of our resistance, and thereby to *widen* our channels of receptivity to Him? And would not His infinite wisdom then, like the ocean, flow into us more abundantly?

If this was true, then, obviously, we should seek above all to develop ourselves, not in worldly ways — esthetically or intellectually or pragmatically — but spiritually, by developing that aspect of our nature which is closest to God, so that He might enter into and enlighten our consciousness. If we begin there, then perhaps the Divine Ocean will actually assist us to broaden our mental channels.

I realized now that religion is far more than a system of beliefs, and far more than a formalized effort to wheedle a little pity out of God by offering Him pleading, self-condemning prayers and propitiatory rites. If our link with Him lies in the fact that we manifest Him already, *then it is up to us to receive Him ever more perfectly, to express Him ever more fully.** And *this* is what religion is all about! True religion consists of *a growing awareness of our deep,*

---

*"But as many as *received* him, to them gave he power to become the sons of God." (John 1:12) *spiritual relationship with God*! What I had seen thus far of religious practices, and turned away from in disappointment, was not religion *definitively practiced*, but the merest toddling first steps on a stairway to the stars! One might, I reflected, devote his entire life to such religion and still have an eternity of development to look forward to. What a thrilling prospect!

This, then, was my calling in life: I would seek God!

Dazed with the grandeur of my reflections, I hardly knew how or at what hour I found my way home again. "Home" at this time was a large, five-room apartment on South Battery which I shared with four of my fellow drama students. On my return there I found them seated, chatting in the kitchen. More or less automatically, I joined them for a cup of coffee. But my thoughts were far from that convivial gathering. So overwhelmed was I by my new insights that I could hardly speak.

"Look at Don! What's there to be so solemn about?" When they found that I couldn't, or wouldn't, participate in their merriment, their laughter assumed a note of mockery.

"Don keeps trying to solve the riddle of the universe! Yuk! Yuk! Yuk!"

"Ah, sweet mystery of life!" crooned another.

"Why, can't you see?" reasoned the fourth, addressing me. "It's all so simple! There's no riddle to be solved! Just get drunk when you like, have fun, shack up with a girl whenever you can, and forget all this craziness!"

"Yeah," reiterated the first, heavily. "Forget it."

"Who Am I? What Is God?"

To my state of mind just then my roommates sounded like yapping puppies. Of what use to me, such friends? I went quietly to my room.

A few days later I was discussing religion with another acquaintance.

"If you want spiritual teachings," he remarked suddenly, "you'll find all your answers in the *Bhagavad Gita*."

"What's that?" Somehow I found this foreign name strangely appealing.

"It's a Hindu Scripture."

Hindu? And what was *that*? I knew nothing of Indian philosophy. This name, however, the *Bhagavad Gita*, lingered with me.

If religion was a matter of becoming more receptive to God, it was high time, I decided, that I got busy and did what I could to make myself receptive. But how? It wasn't that I had no idea how to improve myself. Rather, I saw so much room for improvement that I hardly knew where to begin.

There was the question of my psychological faults: intellectual pride, an overly critical nature. No one, myself included, was happy with these traits in me. But how was I to work on them? And for that matter, were they entirely unmixed evils? Was it wrong, for instance, to *think*? Was it wrong to stand honestly by the fruits of one's thinking, regardless of the opinions of others? And was it so wrong to be critical of attitudes that one's discrimination declared to be false? People who were more concerned for their own comfort than for my spiritual development condemned these traits in me outright. But to me it seemed that there were aspects of my very faults that must be deemed virtues. How was I to sift one from the other?

Contemplating my more socially admissible virtues, I saw that the very opposite was true: In some ways these assumed the nature of faults. My compassion for the sufferings of others, for example, prompted me to try to help them beyond my own capabilities. How else to account for my desire to help them through my writings, when I didn't even know what to write? Here again: How was I to sift truth from error?

Was there *any* way out of my psychological labyrinth?

Even on a physical level, the possibilities for self-improvement seemed bewilderingly complex. I read in a magazine advertisement the names of several famous people who had been vegetarians. *Vegetarians?* Was it really desirable, or even possible, to live without eating meat? Again, I read somewhere else that white flour is harmful to the health. *White flour?*

Heretofore, a hamburger on a white bun, decorated with a thin sliver of tomato and a limp wisp of lettuce, had been my idea of a balanced meal. It seemed now that there were all sorts of opinions on even so basic a subject as diet.

Finally, bewildered by the sheer number of the choices before me, I decided that there could be but one way out of my imperfections: God. I must let *Him* guide my life. I must leave off seeking human solutions, and give up defining my search in terms of human relations.

And what of my plans to be a playwright? Well,

what had I been writing, anyway? Could I who knew nothing, say anything meaningful to anyone else? I had deluded myself for a time with the thought that perhaps, if I were vague enough, I might write works with cryptic messages that others would understand, even if I myself had no idea what those messages were. But now I realized that in this thought, common as it is among writers, I had not been honest. No, I must give up writing altogether. I must give up my plans to flood the world with my ignorance. Surely, out of very compassion for people I must leave off trying to help them. I must renounce their world, their interests, their attachments, their pursuits. I must seek God in the wilderness, in the mountains, in complete solitude.

I would become a hermit.

And what was it I hoped to find, once I made this renunciation? Peace of mind? Inner strength, perhaps? A little happiness?

Wistfully I thought: happiness! I recalled the pure happiness I had known as a child, and lost in the pseudo-sophistication of my youth. Would I ever find it again? Only, I thought, if I became simple once again, like a child. Only if I forsook overintellectuality, and became utterly open to God's love.

I pursued this line of thinking for a time, when a new kind of doubt seized me: Was I losing my mind? Whoever had heard of anyone actually seeking God? Whoever had heard of anyone communing with Him? Was I completely lunatic, to be dreaming of blazing trails where none had ventured before? For I knew nothing as yet about the lives of saints. Vaguely I'd heard them described as people who lived close to God, but the mental image I'd formed of them was of no more than ordinarily good people who went about smiling at children, doing kind deeds, and murmuring, "*Pax vobiscum,*" or some such pious formula, whenever anybody got in their way. What demon of presumption was possessing me that I should be dreaming of actually *finding* God? Surely, I *must* be going mad!

Yet, if this *were* madness, was it not a more solacing condition than the world's vaunted "sanity"? For it was a madness that promised hope, in a world bereft of hope. It was a madness that promised peace, in a world of conflict and warfare. It was a madness that promised happiness, in a world of suffering, cynicism, and broken dreams.

I knew not how to take even my first steps toward God, but my longing for Him had by now become almost obsessive.

Where could I turn? To whom could I look for guidance? The religious people I had met, the monks and ministers, had seemed quite as lost in ignorance as I was.

It occurred to me that I might find in the Scriptures a wisdom those men had overlooked. At least I must *try*.

And what of my plans to become a hermit? That path, surely, I must follow also. Ah! but where? how? with what money to purchase life's essentials? with what practical knowledge to build, plant food, and otherwise fend for myself? Was I not, after all, a mere fool dreaming impractical dreams? Surely, if practical steps had to be taken, there must be more pragmatic solution to my dilemma than drifting off to an existence for which I was utterly untrained.

At this point, Reason stepped onto the scene briskly to resolve my dilemma.

"There's nothing wrong with you," it asserted, "that vigorous, healthful country living can't cure. You've been spending too much time with jaded city people. Get out among simple, genuine, *good* country folk if you want to find peace of mind. Don't waste your life on impossible dreams. Get back to the land! It isn't God you want; it's a more natural way of life, in the harmony and simplicity of Nature."

Ease, in fact, not simplicity, was the heart of this message. For God is so mighty a challenge that the ego will cling to amost anything, rather than heed the call to utter self-surrender.

And, weakling that I was, I relented. I would heed Reason's counsel, I decided. I would go off to the country, commune with Nature, and live among more *natural* human beings.

Chapter Thirteen

A Search for Guide-Maps

MY DECISION TO SEEK peace of mind in an environment of bucolic simplicity coincided with the end of the school year, and the closing of the Dock Street Theater for the summer. I returned to New York.

Dad had recently been posted to Cairo, Egypt, as Esso's exploration manager there. Our home in Scarsdale was let, and mother had taken a house temporarily in White Plains, preparatory to departing for Cairo in August to join Dad. I stayed with her two or three weeks.

My plans for the summer were already set. I said nothing of them, however, to anyone, giving out only that I was going to upstate New York; my spiritual longings I kept a carefully guarded secret. But I put in effect immediately my plan to study the Scriptures. Borrowing Mother's copy of the Holy Bible, I began reading it from the beginning.

"In the beginning God created the heaven and the earth .... And God said, let there be light: and there was light." Who is not familiar with these wonderful lines?

"And the LORD God planted a garden eastward in Eden; and there he put the man whom he had formed ... And the LORD God commanded the man, saying, Of every tree of the garden thou mayest freely eat: But of the tree of the knowledge of good and evil, thou shalt not eat of it: for in the day that thou eatest thereof thou shalt surely die."

But — what was this? How could God possibly want man to *remain* ignorant?

And so man ate the fruit, became wise, and was forced in consequence to live like a witless serf. What kind of teaching was this?

Chapter Five: Here I learned that Adam lived nine hundred and thirty years; his son, Seth, nine hundred and twelve years, and Seth's son, Enos, nine hundred and five years. Cainan, Enos's son, "lived seventy years, and begat Mahalaleel: and Cainan lived after he begat Mahalaleel eight hundred and forty years, and begat sons and daughters: And all the days of Cainan were nine hundred and ten years: and he died. And Mahalaleel lived sixty and five years, and begat Jared ... And Jared lived an hundred sixty and two years, and he begat Enoch ... And Enoch lived sixty and five years, and begat Methuselah ... And all the days of Methuselah were nine hundred sixty and nine years: and he died."

What in heaven's name did it all mean? Was some deep symbolism involved.* All this said nothing whatever to my present needs. Disappointed, I put the book down.

Over the years since then, a number of well-meaning Christians have sought to persuade me that God's truth can be found only in the Bible. If this were true, I cannot imagine that one who was seeking as sincerely as I was would have been turned away at the very threshold by what he read in the Good Book itself. It wasn't until I met my guru, and learned from *him* the teachings of the Bible, that I was able to return to it with a sense of real appreciation. For the time being, I'm afraid I simply bogged down in the "begats."

In Mother's library there was another book that captured my interest. This one contained brief excerpts from the major religions of the world. Perhaps here I would find the guidance I was seeking.

The selections from the Bible in this book proved more meaningful to me, but even so they seemed too anthropomorphic for my tastes, steeped as I was in the scientific view of reality. The Judaic, the Moslem, the Taoist, the Buddhist, the Zoroastrian — all, I found poetically beautiful and inspiring, but for me still there was something lacking. I was being asked to believe, but none of these Scriptures, as nearly as I could tell, was asking me to *experience*. Without actual experience of God, what was the good of mere belief? The farther I read, the more all

---

*Later, when I read my guru's explanation of the story of Adam and Eve, I found its inner meaning profound and deeply inspiring.

of these Scriptures impressed me as — well, great, no doubt, but at last hopelessly beyond me. Perhaps it was simply a question of style. The standard language of Scripture, I reflected, was cryptic to the point of being incomprehensible.

And then I came upon excerpts from the Hindu teachings — a few pages only, but what a revelation! Here the emphasis was on cosmic realities. God was described as an Infinite Consciousness; man, as a manifestation of that consciousness. Why, this was the very concept I myself had worked out on that long evening walk in Charleston! Man's highest duty, I read, is to attune himself with that divine consciousness: Again, this was what I had worked out! Man's ultimate goal, according to these writings, is to experience that divine reality *as his true Self*. But how scientific! What infinite promise! Poetic symbolism abounded here, too, as in the other Scriptures, but here I found also explanations, crystal clear and logical. Best of all, I found advice: not only on the religious life generally, but more specifically, on *how to seek God*.

All this was exactly what I'd been seeking! I felt like a poor man who has just been given a priceless gift. Hastily I skimmed through these excerpts; then, realizing the awesome importance they held for me, I put the book aside, and resolved to wait for a later time when I would be free to read these teachings slowly and digest them. Casually I asked Mother if I might take the book upstate with me for the summer. "Of course," she replied, never suspecting the depth of my interest.

My Aunt Alleen, Mother's half-sister, visited us

in White Plains during my stay there. Sensing the turmoil seething within me, she remarked to Mother one day, "I bet Don ends up in a theological seminary."

"Oh, not *Don!*" Mother's tone implied, "almost anyone else." The change in my life, when it came, caught her completely by surprise.

Two or three times during my stay in White Plains I took the train into New York City, and there contemplated anew the unending throng of tense, worried faces. How many human tragedies were written there in lines of desperation, of bitterness, of hidden grief! More keenly than ever I felt the bond of our common humanity. The worst criminal, I reflected, might have been I. For who was safe from ignorance? Doubtless even the drug addict felt justified in the attitudes that had drawn him into his web of confusion. What, then, of my own present attitudes? Did I dare trust them? How could anyone, at any given hour in his life, know *for a certainty* that his most well-intentioned behavior would advance him toward freedom, and not enmesh him in further bondage? My growing conviction that everything is a part of one Reality, while it gave me a deep sense of kinship with others, awakened in me at the same time a terrifying sense of my own vulnerability. I visualized myself drifting through skies of ignorance in which it was as much my potential to fall as to rise.

It was high time, surely, that I took my own life in hand. Too long had I been floating about haphazardly on seas of circumstance, vaguely hoping that my general direction would be toward the shores of truth, I must begin now to direct my life consciously.

One afternoon I was walking down Fifth Avenue. The heat was oppressive. A bar, cool and inviting, stood before me on a street corner. I stepped in and had a couple of refreshing beers. Though not intoxicated, I realized that my reflexes were not quite as keen as they had been when I came in. I'd never considered drinking a personal problem, nor had I seen anything wrong with drinking in moderation. But it occurred to me now that if anything could lessen my self-control even to this small degree, I would be wise to avoid it. On leaving that barroom I resolved never again to take another drink. Nor have I ever done so.

My trip upstate New York had been intended, originally, to help me find peace without effort, amid the beauties of Nature. But by the time I left White Plains my resolution to work on myself had stiffened markedly, encouraged by the brief excerpts I had read from the Indian Scriptures. Having given up drinking — and also, two or three months previously, smoking — I was beginning to feel an actual enthusiasm for self-discipline. I still hoped that more natural surroundings would contribute something to my peace of mind, but I had no illusions that all my answers would be found in a random assortment of hills and trees. God saw to it, as I shall explain later on, that *none* of my answers were found there.

As a start toward self-transformation, I decided to begin with vigorous physical discipline. In my initial enthusiasm, of course, I overdid it.

The Search

I set out on a one-speed bicycle, taking with me a knapsack that contained only Mother's book of Scriptural excerpts, a few clothes, and a poncho. I had no sleeping bag; absurd as it may seem, I knew nothing of proper camping procedures; I wasn't even aware that there *were* such things as sleeping bags.

My first night I spent in an open field, the poncho spread out underneath me as protection against the damp earth. At three in the morning I awoke, freezing cold, to find myself sloshing about in a puddle of water, collected by my poncho from the heavy dew. Further sleep proved impossible. After some time I got up, resignedly, and started bicycling again. Mile followed weary mile through deserted mountain terrain, scarcely a village in sight anywhere. Toward afternoon the seat of my bicycle felt so hard that, even though I tried softening it with a folded towel, I could hardly bear to sit down. After ten or twelve hours of ceaseless pedaling, my legs, unaccustomed to this strenuous effort, felt with every upgrade that they must shortly give out altogether. Towards later afternoon I watched hopefully for signs of a village with an inn, for on one point I was resolved: I would not, if I could possibly help it, sleep in another field. But I saw not a house. Sixteen hours I pedaled that day, mostly uphill, on my one-speed bicycle; I covered well over a hundred miles.

The sun was low in the west when I met a hiker who informed me that there was a village two miles or so off the road I was on, and that that village had a guest house. With very nearly my last ounce of strength I pedaled there. In the center of the village

A Search for Guide-Maps

I found a house in front of which stood the reassuring sign, "Rooms for Rent." Literally staggering inside, I collapsed in a chair by the front door.

"May I please have a room?"

"Oh, I'm *so* sorry. We've been meaning to take that sign down. We no longer rent rooms."

Despair seized me. "Is there no place nearby where I could spend the night?"

"Well, there's an inn down the road about a mile. I'm sure they'd have a room for you."

A whole mile! Even this short distance was too great for me, in my present state of exhaustion; I hardly had strength enough left to stand. "Please, do you think you might phone and ask them to come fetch me in their car?"

A ride was arranged. That night in bed I actually thought I might die. I didn't realize it at the time, but since early childhood I had had a minor heart condition. That entire night my heart pounded on the walls of my chest as though it would break them. I slept around the clock. Mercifully, by mid-morning my heartbeat had returned to normal. Feeling refreshed, though sore in every muscle, I was eager to continue my journey.

An important passage in the *Bhagavad Gita*, which unfortunately I had yet to read, counsels moderation in all things.* I had discovered the merits of this precept quite on my own! From now on, I decided, I'd better proceed on the pathway to perfection at a more measured pace. I must tighten the screw carefully, lest it split the wood.

And so I proceeded, this time more slowly, to the small mountain town of Indian Lake, where I rented

The Search

a room and settled eagerly to my reward: a careful study of the few excerpts I had from the Indian Scriptures.

> * But for earthly needs
> Religion is not his who too much fasts
> Or too much feasts, nor his who sleeps away
> An idle mind; nor his who wears to waste
> His strength in vigils. Nay, Arjuna call
> That the true piety which most removes
> Earth-aches and ills, where one is moderate
> In eating and in resting, and in sport;
> Measured in wish and act; sleeping betimes,
> Waking betimes for duty.
> —*Bhagavad Gita*, in Sir Edwin Arnold's
> translation, *The Song Celestial.*

Chapter Fourteen

Joy Is Inside!

"Perfect bliss
Grows only in the bosom tranquillised,
The spirit passionless, purged from offense,
Vowed to the Infinite. He who thus vows
His soul to the Supreme Soul, quitting sin,
Passes unhindered to the endless bliss
Of unity with Brahma."

READING THESE WORDS from the *Bhagavad Gita*, my imagination was deeply stirred. The task I faced, as I was learning from the excerpts before me, was to calm my thoughts and feelings, to make myself an open and empty receptacle for God's grace. If I did so, so these teachings stated, God would enter my life and fill it.

How different these simple precepts from the meandering theology that I had heard proclaimed from pulpits on Sunday mornings! Here I found no beggarly self-abasement — the weak man's masquerade of humility; no talk of the importance of entering a religious institution as a doorway to heaven; no effort to hold God at a distance with the diplomatic address of formal prayer; no hint at compromising one's spiritual commitment by concern over its social acceptability. What I read here was fresh, honest, and convincing. It gave me extraordinary hope.

One thing that had disturbed me about all the churches I'd visited was their sectarianism. "Ours is the one, the only true way" was a dogma implied even when it wasn't stated. Invariably it suggested that all other ways were false, that even if other groups loved the same God, *their* message, in some indiscernible manner, was "of the devil."

How different were the teachings I was reading now! All paths, according to them, lead by various routes to the same, infinite goal. "As a mother," one stated, "in nursing her sick children, gives rice and curry to one, sago and arrowroot to another, and bread and butter to a third, so the Lord has laid out different paths for different men, suitable to their natures."

How beautiful! How persuasive in its utter fairness!

Another point that had always troubled me in my contacts with the churches was their ministers' tendency to discourage questioning. "Have faith," they told me. But what sort of "faith" is it that refuses to submit itself to honest challenges? Could the motive behind such refusal be anything but what it seems on the surface: fear? Fear that one's beliefs were a house built on sand? Even in their efforts to be reasonable, those ministers wore blinders, for while they quoted Scripture to support their beliefs, they never admitted the possibility that those very quotations might have other meanings than those they ascribed to them. Even the closest disciples of Jesus were often scolded by him for mistaking his true meanings. Is it, then, wise and humble for us, who live so far from him in time, to insist that *we* understand him better? The Scriptures are intended to expand our understanding, not to suffocate it.

But then, as my guru later pointed out to me, one difference between recorded Scriptures and a living teacher is that the seeker's misunderstandings cannot be rebutted, patiently or sharply as the occasion demands, by the pages of a book.

The Indian teachings, unlike those ministers I had known, stressed the need for testing every Scriptural claim. Direct, personal experience of God, not dogmatic or uncritical belief, was the final test they proposed, but they also suggested intermediate tests by which the veriest beginner would know whether he was headed in the right direction, and not slipping off into one of life's innumerable detours.

I had already realized from my own experience that the difference between a right decision and a wrong one can be subtle. I was impressed therefore with teachings that can be verified not only after death, but here on earth, in this lifetime.*

---

*The Bible, too, stresses verification by actual experience. "Test the spirits," wrote St. John in his first epistle. Religionists who empha-

These were the teachings for which I had longed. Yes, I vowed again, I would dedicate my life to seeking God! Too long had I delayed, too long vacillated with doubts, too long sought earthly, not divine solutions to the deepest problems of life. Art? Science? New social structures? What could any of these things do to lift man high, or for very long? Without inner transformation, any outer improvement in the human lot would be like trying to strengthen a termite-ridden building with a fresh coat of paint.

One parable in the reading I was engaged in affected me especially. It was from the sayings of a great saint of the Nineteenth Century, Sri Ramakrishna. Not knowing who he was, I imagined the saying was taken from some ancient Scripture.

"How," Sri Ramakrishna asked, "does a man come to have dispassion? A wife once said to her husband, 'Dear, I am very anxious about my brother. For the past one week he has been thinking of becoming an ascetic, and is making preparations for it. He is trying to reduce gradually all his desires and wants.' The husband replied, 'Dear, be not at all anxious about your brother. He will never become a Sannyasin. No one can become a Sannyasin in that way.' 'How does one become a Sannyasin, then?' asked the wife. 'It is done in this way!' the husband exclaimed. So saying, he tore into pieces his flowing dress, took a piece out of it, tied it round his loins, and told his wife that she and all others of her sex were thenceforth mothers to him. He left the house,

size blind belief until death generally haven't tasted the fruits of the religious life themselves, because they haven't practiced it.

Joy Is Inside!

never more to return."*

The courage of this man's renunciation stirred me to the depths. By contrast, how I had vacillated in my doubts!

All these excerpts were saying but one thing in essence: that perfection must be sought within the self, not in the outer world. Of the truth of this teaching God evidently had it in mind to give me abundant proof that summer.

Indian Lake is a beautiful place of pine trees and cool forest glades, of rolling hills and gently rippling water. "If I'm to relate more deeply to cosmic realities," I thought, "I could begin in no better place than right here." Indeed, the very scenery invited communion. I tried consciously to *feel* the thrill of a raindrop as it quivered on a pine needle; the exquisite freshness of the morning dew; the burst of sunlight through the clouds at sunset. Always I had loved Nature, and felt deeply drawn to her beauty in woods, lakes, flowers, and starry skies. But now, as I endeavored to intensify my sensitivity, *to enter directly* into the life all around me, I discovered with a pang what an utter prisoner I was, locked in my own ego. I could see; I could not *feel*. Or, to the extent that I *could* feel, it was on only with a small part of me, not with my whole being. I was like an eight-

---

*This story has to be understood in its own cultural context. Marital fidelity is highly regarded in India. The Hindu Scriptures state, however, that that which is otherwise a duty ceases to be such when it conflicts with a higher duty. The highest duty of mankind is to seek God. It is understood in India that one's spouse can and should be supportive in this search. Only if the desire for God is intense, and one's spouse, by his or her worldliness, poses an obstacle to that search, would it be permissible to break that marital tie without mutual consent.

cylinder motor hitting on only one cylinder. Surely if even here, in these perfect surroundings, I could not rise out of myself and attune myself with greater realities, no mere *place* would ever accomplish such a transformation for me. Obviously, it was I, myself, who needed changing. Whether my outer environment was beautiful or ugly was not particularly significant. What mattered was what I made of my own inner "environment" of thoughts, feelings, and inspirations.

I now was spending some time every day in meditation. I didn't know how to go about it, but believed that if I could only calm my mind a little bit, I would at least be headed in the right direction. I prayed daily, too: something I hadn't had faith enough to do until now.

For my outer life God was, I suspect, saying to me with a friendly chuckle, "You expected to find a better type of humanity in the country? Take a look around you! Man is not better for *where* he lives. Dreams of outer perfection are a delusion. Happiness must be found inside or it will not be found anywhere!"

My first plan for a job at Indian Lake had been to work as a lumberjack. I asked my landlady what she thought of my chances of finding such employment.

"What!" she cried. "And get knifed in a drunken brawl? Those men aren't your type at all."

Well, I had to admit her description left something to be desired. But I wasn't to be put off so easily. For two days I trudged about in the woods, looking for a logging camp that was said to be in the vicinity. Perhaps it was God's will that I missed it; at any rate, all I encountered were swarms of deer flies. Covered with stings, I found myself more receptive the third day to my landlady's warnings. I decided to seek employment elsewhere.

That morning a local farmer agreed to hire me as a handyman. I'd had a little experience with farm work just after graduation from high school, and had enjoyed it then. But never before had I worked for such a man as this. My intention was to work quietly, thinking of God. But my employer had other, to him infinitely better, ideas: He wanted me to play the fool in his little kingdom. "What else is a handyman for?" he demanded rhetorically, when I remonstrated at being made the constant butt of his rustic jokes. Humor I didn't mind, but I drew the line at *witless* humor. There are few things so exasperating as meeting a gibe with a clever thrust, only to have it soar yards over the other person's head. When, after a few clever sallies, I lapsed resignedly into silence, the farmer teased, "C'mon, flannelmouth! I hired you to *work*. Don't stand there jabbering all day." And that, as I recall, was the high point of his comedy routine. My image of the genuine, innocent, *good* rustic was beginning to fade.

I soon left this worthy's employ. Putting peaceful Indian Lake resolutely behind me, I set off down the road on my bicycle in search of other work. Hours later I came to a mine owned by the Union Carbide Corporation. There the hiring clerk looked at me dubiously.

"We have work, all right," she said, "but it isn't your kind of work."

"What do you mean, not my kind of work? I can

do anything!"

"Well, you won't like this job. You'll see. You won't last a week." With that encouragement I was hired.

The atmosphere of the sintering plant, where I was employed, was so thick with the dust of the ore they were mining that one couldn't even see across the room. At the end of every day my face and hands were completely black. Some idea was beginning to form in my mind of what the woman had meant.

But it wasn't the work itself that finally got to me. It was another of those simple, genuine, innocent, *good* rustics — a complete fool who, finding me too polite to tell him, as everyone else did, to go to hell, mistook me for an even greater fool than himself. All day, every day, he regaled me with lies about his heroic feats before, during, and after World War II. Then, taking my silence for credulity, he began preening himself on his own superior intelligence. Finally he informed me disdainfully that I was too stupid to be worthy of association with one of his own incomparable brilliance.

The hiring clerk didn't even trouble to remind me of her prediction, when I appeared after a week for my severance pay.

How, I wondered, would I ever become a hermit? A person needed money to buy food. Probably I'd have to find employment from time to time merely to stay alive. But if these were samples of the kind of work I'd find out in the country, I wasn't so sure that my spiritual losses wouldn't outweigh the gains. Perhaps, I thought, if I could find some place where the money I earned could be stretched farther...

That was it! I would go to some part of the world where the cost of living was low: yes, to south America. I would work in this country first, and save up. It wouldn't cost much, surely, to get to South America; perhaps I could even work my way down there. And there I'd find it possible to live a long time on my savings — years even, perhaps, meditating in some secluded jungle spot, or on a mountaintop. My problem, now, was how to earn as much money as possible in the shortest possible time.

At the mine, one of my co-workers had entertained me after work with tales of the huge earnings he'd accumulated one summer in tips as a bellhop at a resort hotel. The thought of milking people by doing special favors for them was odious to me, but perhaps, I thought, if I kept my goal firmly in mind, I would be able to suppress my distaste.

My next stop was the resort town of Lake George. Coming to a hotel, I approached the owner and asked if he was in need of a bellhop.

"Got one already." He eyed me speculatively. "Where you from?"

"Scarsdale."

"Oh, Scarsdale, eh?" His eyes flickered with interest. "Wouldn't hurt to have someone from Scarsdale working here." He paused. "Okay, you're on."

Well, by no stretch of the imagination could *this* fellow be called a rustic! He was first, last, and forever a shyster in the art of turning little fortunes into big ones. His guests received as little from him as possible in return for everything he could squeeze out of them. The janitor and cleaning woman were his first cousins, emigrants from Europe, but he treated them like serfs. When I saw him for what he was, it shamed me to be working for him. And it shamed me almost more to accept tips from the guests, whom it was my pleasure to serve. When one couple tried to tip me a second time for fetching something else from their car, I simply couldn't accept their offer. Hardly a week after my arrival I was off down the road again.

The time was approaching in any case for me to return to White Plains and help Mother make preparations for her voyage to Egypt.

My trip south held a certain hope also. A coworker at the mine had suggested that I might get a job in the merchant marine, where the veriest beginner earned as much as $300 a month. This was good pay in those days. Better still, since I would be out at sea, receiving free board and lodging, I'd be able to save quite a lot of money quickly. I decided to try my luck before the mast.

The summer so far had proved a mixed bag: uplifting in the truths I had learned, but materially a fiasco. More and more I was coming to feel as though I had landed on the wrong planet. None of my experiences these past months had helped me to feel at home here.

Yet my desire to "drop out" seemed, from every practical standpoint, wildly unrealistic. I could not but admit to myself that my plans for becoming a hermit rested on the shakiest possible ground. I knew nothing of the practical skills I'd need to live alone in the wilderness. I had no idea how much money I'd actually require to remain in South America a long time. Worst of all, I knew so little of the spiritual path that I had no confidence in my ability to walk it alone. I didn't know how to meditate. I didn't know how to pray. I didn't know what to think about through the day when I wasn't meditating or praying. I was beginning to realize that, without guidance, I was as good as lost.

Yet I knew of no one whom I could trust to guide me out of the empty corridors of institutional religion into the free air of universal truth. I was contemplating a path that seemed, from every practical viewpoint, sheer folly. But I was doing so because I had ruled out every conceivable alternative.

The thought of living a so-called "normal," worldly life filled me with anguish, the more so because I felt so alone in my rejection of it. Most of my friends were getting married, and settling down into good jobs. The pressure on me — from them, and from society — to do likewise was, in a sense, constant. But to my mind, even a lifetime of starvation and suffering would be worth it, if only by so living I could find God.

And what did I hope to achieve in finding Him? There, my notions remained vague, though certainly I would have considered even peace of mind an incomparable blessing. But what mattered to me was that to know Him would be to know Reality, and that not knowing Him meant embracing falsehood and delusion. Wherever my path led, I knew I had but one valid choice: to offer my life to Him. Thereafter, it would be up to Him to lead me where He would.

Chapter Fifteen

A Map Discovered

AS SOON AS POSSIBLE after my return to White Plains I went to Bowling Green in New York City, and applied for a merchant mariner's card. This I received on August 24th with the classification, "Ordinary seaman, messman, wiper." Thereafter I was told it was only a question of waiting for a ship that would give me a berth. My hope was to ship out as soon as possible.

Meanwhile I helped Mother pack. When her sailing date came, I accompanied her to the dock in New York and saw her off safely. Next I went down to Bowling Green to see if any ships had come in. No luck: "Come back in a few days." With most of the afternoon still before me, I went uptown to browse at Brentano's, the famous Fifth Avenue bookstore.

A Map Discovered

At Brentano's I got into a discussion on spiritual matters with a sales clerk, who showed me a few books by Thomas Merton, the young Protestant Christian who converted to Roman Catholicism, then went on to become a Trappist monk. I was intrigued, though I didn't feel personally attracted. It was the catholicity — which is to say, the *universality* — of India's teachings that had won my devotion.

From Brentano's I went up Fifth Avenue to another book store: Doubleday-Doran, as it was named then. Here I found an entire section of books on Indian philosophy — the first I had ever seen. Hungrily I feasted my gaze on the wide variety of titles: The *Upanishads*, the *Bhagavad Gita*, the *Ramayana*, the *Mahabharata*, books on yoga. I finished scanning these shelves, then turned back to go over them once again. This time, to my surprise, the first book I saw, standing face outward on the shelf, was one I hadn't even noticed the first time. The author's photograph on the cover affected me strangely. Never had I met anyone whose face radiated so much goodness, humility, and love. Eagerly I picked up the book and glanced again at its title:

Autobiograpy of a Yogi, by Paramhansa Yogananda. The author lived in America — in California! Was this someone at last who could *help* me in my search? As I started to leaf through the book, these words caught my attention: "Dedicated to the memory of Luther Burbank, an American saint."

An American *saint*? But, how preposterous! How could anyone become a saint in this land of the "almighty dollar"? this materialistic desert? this ... I closed the book in dismay, returning it to its place on the shelf.

That day I bought my first book of Indian philosophy — not *Autobiography of a Yogi*, but Sir Edwin Arnold's beautiful translation of the *Bhagavad Gita*. Eagerly I took this treasure home with me to Scarsdale, where I had temporarily rented a private room. For the next couple of days I fairly devoured it, feeling as though I were soaring in vast skies of pure wisdom.

> "By this sign is [the sage] known
> Being of equal grace to comrades, friends,
> Chance-comers, strangers, lovers, enemies,
> Aliens and kinsmen; loving all alike,
> Evil or good."

What wonderful words! Thrilled, I read on:

> "Yea, knowing Me the source of all, by Me
>   all creatures wrought,
> The wise in spirit cleave to Me, into My
>   being brought ...
> And unto these — thus serving well, thus
>   loving ceaselessly —
> I give a mind of perfect mood, whereby they
>   draw to Me;
> And, all for love of them, within their darkened
>   souls I dwell,
> And, with bright rays of wisdom's lamp, their
>   ignorance dispell."

My own doubts, too, were being dispelled by

these marvelous teachings. I knew now with complete certainty that this path was right for me.

The day after I finished my first reading of the *Bhagavad Gita*, I returned to New York, intending to visit Bowling Green and see if any ship had come in. I was walking down Seventh Avenue toward the subway, the entrance to which was on the far side of the next cross street, when I recalled the book I'd rejected so summarily on my last visit to the city: *Autobiography of a Yogi*. As I remembered that beautiful face on the cover, a strong urge from within prompted me to go buy it. I thrust the thought firmly out of my mind.

"That isn't what I'm looking for," I told myself. Chuckling, I added, "An American saint, indeed!" Resolutely I continued walking toward the subway.

"How can you know what the book's really like, if you won't even read it?" came the urge again, not with words, but with unmistakable meaning.

"No!" I repeated. I then offered reasons: "I've got to stop reading books; I'm too intellectual as it is. Besides, if I'm ever to become a hermit, I'm going to have to *save* money, not continually spend it!"

At that moment I reached the corner. I was proceeding toward the curb ahead of me when I felt as though an actual force were turning me left around the corner, and propelling me toward Fifth Avenue. I'd never experienced anything like it before. Amazed, I asked myself, "Is there something in this book that I'm *meant* to read?" Resisting no longer, I hastened eagerly in the direction of Doubleday-Doran's.

Entering the store, I made straight for the book

The Search

and bought it. As I was turning to leave, I bumped into Doug Burch, that friend from my Scarsdale High School days who had introduced me to Nick's and dixieland jazz. We exchanged news briefly. Doug began describing to me in glowing terms his plans for making a career in radio and advertising. The longer he talked, the more closely I hugged my increasingly precious new book to my heart. Imperceptibly, my doubts about it had already vanished. I felt as though Yogananda were sharing my dismay at the shining prospects Doug was describing, a way of life that, to me, spelled desolation. Holding the book, I felt suddenly as though this oriental yogi and I were old friends. The world and I were strangers, but here was one who knew me, and understood.

I waited until I reached my room in Scarsdale before opening the book. And then began the most thrilling literary adventure of my life.

Autobiography of a Yogi is the story of a young Indian's intense search for God. It describes a number of living saints that he met on his journey, including his great guru, Swami Sri Yukteswar. It also describes, more clearly than any other mystical work I have ever read, the author's own experiences with God, including the highest one possible, *samadhi*, or mystical union. In chapter after chapter I found moving testimony to God's *living* reality, not only in the abstraction of infinity, but in the hearts and lives of actual human beings. I read of how Yogananda's prayers even for little things had been answered, and of how, by placing himself unreservedly in God's hands, his unanticipated needs had always been met. I read of intense love for God such as I myself yearned to possess; of a relationship with the Lord more intimate, more dear than I had dared to imagine possible.

Until now I had supposed that a life of devotion might give one, at best, a little peace of mind. But here, suddenly, I discovered that the fruit of spiritual living is a joy beyond human imagination!

Until recently I had doubted the value of prayer, except perhaps as a means of uplifting *oneself*. But now I learned, and could not for a moment doubt, that God related individually, *lovingly*, to every seeker.

Miracles abound in this book. Many of these, I confess, were quite beyond my powers of acceptance at the time. But instead of dismissing them, as I would certainly have done if I'd read of them in most other books, I suspended my incredulity. For the spirit of this story was so deeply honest, so transparently innocent of pride or impure motive that it was impossible for me to doubt that its author believed implicitly every word he had written. Never before had I encountered a spirit so clearly truthful, so filled with goodness and joy. Every page seemed radiant with light. Reading *Autobiography of a Yogi*, I alternated between tears and laughter: tears of pure joy; laughter of even greater joy! For three days I scarcely ate or slept. When I walked it was almost on tiptoe, as though in an ecstatic dream.

What this book described, finally, was the highest of sciences, Kriya Yoga, a technique that enables the seeker to advance rapidly on the path of meditation. I, who wanted so desperately to learn how to meditate, felt all the excitement of one who has

The Search

found a treasure map, the treasure in this case being a divine one buried deep within my own self!

Autobiography of a Yogi is the greatest book I have ever read. One perusal of it was enough to change my entire life. From that time on my break with the past was complete. I resolved in the smallest detail of my life to follow Paramhansa Yogananda's teaching.

Finding that he recommended a vegetarian diet, I immediately renounced meat, fish, and fowl. He could have recommended a diet of bread and water and I'd have obeyed him without a qualm.

For, more than anything else, what this book gave me was the conviction that in Yogananda I had found my guru, my spiritual teacher for all time to come. A few days earlier I hadn't even known this strange word, *guru*. I hadn't known anything about yoga, or reincarnation, or karma, or almost any of the basic precepts of Indian philosophy. Now incredibly, I felt such deep, utter trust in another human being that, ignorant though I was of his philosophy, I was willing to follow him to the end of life. And while I had yet to meet him, I felt that he was the truest friend I had ever known.

The day after I became a vegetarian I was invited by friends of my family, Mr. and Mrs. Lloyd Gibson, to lunch at their home. To my combined amusement and dismay, the main dish consisted of chicken à la king. Not wanting to hurt my friends' feelings, I compromised by pushing the chicken bits to one side, and eating the vegetables in their chicken sauce.

George Calvert, on whose father's farm Bob and

A Map Discovered

I had worked after my graduation from high school, had invited me for the following day to lunch at his parents' home, and to a polo game afterwards. This time I had no choice but to refuse the thick, juicy hamburger sandwich that his mother offered me. To make matters more awkward still, George had considerately provided me with a date! I must have seemed strange company indeed, eating hardly anything, and paying as little attention to the girl as politely possible, from the opposite end of the room. (Yogananda was a monk: I, too, would be a monk.) The polo game gave me an opportunity for a little surreptitious meditation, so I didn't view it as a total loss.

Later that day I met my brother Bob and Dean Bassett, a friend of ours, at Nielson's, an ice cream parlor in Scarsdale village. Dean had been voted "biggest wolf" in my senior high school class. He and Bob were discussing Dean's favorite subject: girls.

I listened in silence for a time. At last I protested, "Don't you see? Desire only enslaves one to the very things one desires!"

Bob and Dean gazed at each other quizzically. "What's wrong with him?" Dean asked.

It was years before I realized that comprehension, like a flower, must unfold at its own speed. Until a person is ready for a truth, not even the clearest logic will make it acceptable to him.

As soon as I finished reading *Autobiography of a Yogi*, my impulse was to jump onto the next bus bound for California. Not wanting to act impulsively, however, I waited a whole day! I even debated for several hours whether it might not be wiser for me to go to sea as I'd planned, and there to meditate a few months before making this important decision. But of course I knew already that it *was* the right decision. The following day I packed my bag and took an early train into New York City.

My godfather, Dr. Winthrop Haynes, had been sympathetically concerned for my future. He and his wife were like second parents to me; I didn't feel I could leave New York without bidding him farewell. On my way to the bus station, therefore, I stopped by his office at Rockefeller Center. Finding him not in, I left a note on his desk with the message, "I'm going to California to join a group of people who, I believe, can teach me what I want to know about God and about religion." This was the first intimation I had given anyone that God was my true goal in life.

I took the next westward-bound bus available. Thereafter, for four days and four nights, my home was a succession of buses.

My break with the past was so sudden, so complete that I sometimes ask myself whether some very special grace had not been needed to make it possible. I wonder what I'd have done, for instance, if Mother had still been in America. Would I have had the courage to take this drastic step? I'm not so sure. Very possibly she'd have detained me. And if so, would she have succeeded in deflecting me from my purpose? By this time, of course, the question has become academic, but wasn't it remarkable that I found the book that changed my life less than half a day after I'd put Mother on her ship to Cairo?

Strange indeed are God's ways! I was to see much of them in the years that followed, and never have they ceased to make me marvel.

Chapter Sixteen

The Pilgrim Meets His Guide

I arrived in Los Angeles on the morning of Saturday, September 11, 1948, exhausted from my long journey. There I took advantage of the first opportunity I'd had in four days to shave and bathe, then continued by bus one hundred miles south to Encinitas, the little coastal town where, as I had read, Yogananda had his hermitage. In the fervor of first reading it had somehow eluded me that he had founded a world-wide organization. Perhaps I had subconsciously "tuned out" this information from my longstanding fear of religious institutionalism. In my mind, this little seaside hermitage was all that existed of his work.

I arrived in Encinitas late that afternoon, too tired to proceed at once to the hermitage. I booked

The Pilgrim Meets His Guide

into a hotel and fairly collapsed onto my bed, sleeping around the clock. The next morning I set out for the Self-Realization Fellowship hermitage, walking perhaps a mile past picturesque gardens, colorful with ice plant and bougainvillea. Many of the flowers I saw there were new to me. The vividness of their hues made a vigorous contrast to the more conservative flowers in the East — a contrast, I was to discover, that extended to numerous other aspects of life on the two coasts.

I approached the hermitage with bated breath. Yogananda, I recalled from his book, once visited a saint without sending prior notice that he was coming. He hadn't yet reached the saint's village when the man came out to welcome him. Did Yogananda, too, I asked myself, know I was coming? And would he, too, come out and greet me?

No such luck. I entered the grounds through an attractive gate, to find on both sides of the driveway a large, beautifully kept garden — trees to the left, a wide lawn to the right. At the far end of the driveway stood a lovely white stucco building with a red tile roof. I imagined disciples quietly going about inside, doing simple chores, their faces shining with inner peace. (Did *they* know I was coming?)

I rang the front doorbell. Minutes later a gentle-looking elderly lady appeared.

"May I help you?" she inquired politely.

"Is Paramhansa Yogananda in?"

My pronunciation of this unfamiliar name must have left something to be desired. The white palm beach suit I was wearing, moreover, didn't mark me as the normal visitor. I'd assumed, mistakenly, that palm beach was the accepted attire in southern California, as it was in Miami or Havana. My unusual appearance, together with my obvious unfamiliarity with Yogananda's name, must have given the impression that I was a serviceman of some sort.

"Oh, you've come to check the water?"

"No!" Gulping, I repeated, "Is Paramhansa Yogananda in?"

"Who? Oh, yes, I see. No, I'm afraid he's away for the weekend. Is there anything I can do for you?"

"Well, yes. No. I mean, I wanted to see *him*."

"He's lecturing today at the Hollywood church."

"You have a *church* there?" I'd always imagined that Hollywood consisted of nothing but movie studios. My astonishment must have struck my hostess as unseemly. After all, why *shouldn't* they have a church in a big city like Hollywood? Soon it became apparent to me that I wasn't making the best possible impression.

Well, I thought, perhaps it *did* seem a bit strange, my barging in here and asking to speak to the head of the organization, and — worse still — not even realizing that he *had* an organization. My hostess drew herself up a little stiffly.

"I want to join his work," I explained. "I want to live here."

"Have you studied his printed lessons?" she inquired, a bit coolly I thought.

"Lessons?" I echoed blankly. "I didn't know he had any lessons to be studied." My position seemed to be getting murkier by the minute.

"There's a full course of them. I'm afraid you

The Pilgrim Meets His Guide

couldn't join," she continued firmly, "until after you'd completed the lot."

"How long does that take?" My heart was sinking.

"About four years."

Four years! Why, this was out of the question! As I look back now on that meeting, I think she was probably only trying to temper what, to her, must have seemed my absurd presumption in assuming I had merely to appear on the scene to be welcomed joyously with cries of, "You've arrived!" In fact, the requirement for joining was not so strict as she made it out to be. But it is usual, and also quite proper, for the spiritual aspirant's sincerity to be tested.

It looked less than proper to me at the time, however. It was only later that I learned that my hostess had been Sister Gyanamata, Paramhansa Yogananda's most advanced woman disciple. She herself, it happened, because she had been married, had had to wait years before she could enter the hermitage. The mere *prospect* of a wait must not have seemed to her very much of a test.

Well, I reflected rebelliously, this wasn't *Yogananda's* verdict. Choking down my disappointment, I inquired how I might get to the Hollywood church. Sister Gyanamata gave me the address, and a telephone number. Soon I was on my way back to Los Angeles.

On the way there I alternated between bouts of heated indignation (at *her* presumption!) and desperate prayers for my acceptance. This was the first time in my life I had wanted anything so desperately. I couldn't, I simply *mustn't* be refused.

At one point, thinking again of my elderly hostess, my mind was about to wax indignant once more when suddenly I remembered her eyes. They had been very calm — even, I reflected with some astonishment, wise. Certainly there was far more to her than I'd realized. "Forgive me," I prayed, "for misjudging her. It was wrong of me in any case to think unkindly of her. She was only doing her duty. But I see now that she is a great soul. Forgive me."

A cloud seemed suddenly to lift inside me. I knew in my heart that I'd been accepted.

Arrived in Los Angeles, I checked my bag at the bus depot, and proceeded at once to 4860 Sunset Boulevard, where the church was located. It was about three o'clock in the afternoon. The morning service had long since ended, and, apart from a small scattering of people, the building was empty. A lady greeted me from behind a long table at the back of the room.

"May I help you?"

I explained my mission.

"Oh, I'm afraid you couldn't possibly see him today. His time is completely filled."

I was growing more desperate by the minute. "When *can* I see him?"

She consulted a small book before her on the table. "His appointments are fully booked for the next two and a half months."

Two and a half months! First I'd been told I couldn't join for four years. Now I was told I couldn't even *see* him for ...

"But I've come all the way from New York just

for this!"

"Have you?" She smiled sympathetically. "How did you hear about him?"

"I read his autobiography a few days ago."

"So recently! And you came — just — like that?" She cooled a little. "Usually people write first. Didn't you write?"

Bleakly I confessed I hadn't even thought of doing so.

"Well, I'm sorry, but you can't see him for another two and a half months. In the meantime," she continued, brightening a little, "you can study his lessons, and attend the services here."

Morosely I wandered about the church, studying the furnishings, the architecture, the stained-glass windows. It was an attractive chapel, large enough to seat over one hundred people, and invitingly peaceful. An excellent place, I thought, for quiet meditation. But my own mind was hardly quiet or meditative. It was in turmoil.

"You *must* take me!" I prayed. "You *must*! This means my whole life to me!"

Two or three of the people sitting in the church were monks whose residence was the headquarters of Self-Realization Fellowship on Mt. Washington, in the Highland Park section of Los Angeles. I spoke to one of them. Norman his name was; tall and well-built, his eyes were yet gentle and kind. He talked a little about their way of life at Mt. Washington, and their relation, as disciples, to Paramhansa Yogananda. "We call him, 'Master,'" he told me. From *Autobiography of a Yogi* I knew already that this appellation, which Yogananda used also in reference to his own guru, denoted reverence, not menial subservience.

How Norman's description of Mt. Washington attracted me! I simply *had* to become a part of this wonderful way of life. It was where I belonged. It was my home.

Norman pointed out two young men sitting quietly farther back in the church.

"They want to join, too," he remarked.

"How long have they been waiting?"

"Oh, not long. A few months."

Disconsolately I wandered about awhile longer. Finally it occurred to me — novel thought! — that perhaps I simply wasn't ready, and that for this reason the doors weren't opening for me. If this were true, I decided, I'd just go live in the hills near Hollywood, come to the services regularly, study the lessons, and — I sighed — wait. When I was ready, the Master would know it, and would summon me.

With this resolution in mind, and with no small disappointment in my heart, I made for the door.

No doubt I'd needed this lesson in humility. Perhaps things had always gone too easily for me. Perhaps I was too confident. At any rate, the moment I accepted the thought that I actually might not be spiritually ready, the situation changed dramatically. I had reached the door when the secretary — Mary Hammond, I later learned her name was — came up from behind me.

"Since you've come such a long way," she said, "I'll ask Master if he'd be willing to see you today."

She returned a few minutes later.

"Master will see you next."

Shortly thereafter I was ushered into a small sitting room. The Master was standing there, speaking to a disciple in a white robe. As the young man was about to leave, he knelt to touch the Master's feet. This was, I knew from Yogananda's book, a traditional gesture of reverence among Indians; it is bestowed on parents and other elders as well as on one's guru. A moment later, the Master and I were alone.

What large, lustrous eyes now greeted me! What a compassionate smile! Never before had I seen such divine beauty in a human face. The Master seated himself on a chair, and motioned me to a sofa beside him.

"What may I do for you?" For the third time that day, these same, gentle words. But this time how fraught with meaning!

"I want to be your disciple!" The reply welled up irresistibly from my heart. Never had I expected to utter such words to another human being.

The Master smiled gently. There ensued a long discussion, interspersed by long silences, during which he held his eyes half open, half closed — "reading" me, as I well knew.

Over and over again in my heart I prayed desperately, "You *must* take me! I know that you know my thoughts. I can't say it outwardly; I'd only weep. But you must accept me. You *must*!"

Early in the conversation he told me, "I agreed to see you only because Divine Mother told me to. I want you to know that. It isn't because you've come from so far. Two weeks ago a lady flew here all the way from Sweden after reading my book, but I wouldn't see her. I do only what God tells me to do." He reiterated, "Divine Mother told me to see you."

"Divine Mother," as I already knew from reading his book, was the way he often referred to God, Who, he said, embraces both the male and female principles.

There followed some discussion of my past. He appeared pleased with my replies, and with my truthfulness. "I knew that already," he once remarked, indicating that he was only testing me to see if I would answer him truthfully. Again a long silence, while I prayed ardently to be accepted.

"I am taking fewer people now," he said.

I gulped. Was this remark intended to prepare me for a letdown?

I told him I simply could see nothing for myself in marriage, or in a worldly life. "I'm sure it's fine for many people," I said, "but I don't want it for myself."

He shook his head. "It isn't as fine for *anybody* as people like to make out. God, for everyone, is the *only* answer!" He went on to tell me a few stories of the disillusionments he had witnessed. Then again, silence.

At one point in our discussion he asked me how I had liked his book.

"Oh, it was wonderful!"

"That's because it has my vibrations in it," he replied simply.

Vibrations? I'd never thought of books as possessing "vibrations" before. But, clearly, I had found his book almost alive in its power to convey, not merely ideas, but new states of awareness.

The Pilgrim Meets His Guide

Incongruously, even absurdly, it now occurred to me that he might be more willing to take me if he felt I could be of some practical use to his work. And what did I know? Only writing. But that, surely, was better than nothing. Perhaps he had a need for people with writing skills. To demonstrate my ability, I said:

"Sir, I found several split infinitives in your book." A twenty-two-year-old, literarily untried, but already a budding editor! I've never lived down this faux pas! But Master took it with a surprised, then a humorous, smile. The motive for my remark was transparent to him.

More silence.

More prayers.

"All right," he said at last. "You have good karma. You may join us."

"Oh, but I can wait!" I blurted out, hoping he wasn't taking me only because I hadn't yet found any other place to stay.

"No," he smiled. "You have good karma, otherwise I wouldn't accept you."

Gazing at me with deep love, he then said, "I give you my unconditional love."

Immortal promise! I couldn't begin to fathom the depth of meaning in those marvelous words.

"Will you give me your unconditional love?"

"Yes!"

"And will you also give me your unconditional obedience?"

Desperate though my desire was to be accepted by him, I wanted to be utterly honest. "Suppose," I asked, "sometime, I think you're wrong?"

The Search

"I will never ask anything of you," he replied solemnly, "that God does not tell me to ask." He continued:

"When I met my master, Sri Yukteswar, he said to me, 'Allow me to discipline you.' 'Why, Sir?' I inquired. 'Because,' he answered, 'in the beginning of the spiritual path one's will is guided by whims and fancies. Mine was, too, until I met *my* guru, Lahiri Mahasaya. It was only when I attuned my will to his wisdom-guided will that I found true freedom.' In the same way, if you will tune your will to mine, you, too, will find freedom. To act only on the inspiration of whims and fancies is not freedom, but bondage. Only by doing God's will can you become truly free."

"I see," I replied thoughtfully. Then from my heart I said, "I give you my unconditional obedience!"

My Guru continued: "When I met my master, he gave me his unconditional love as I have given you mine. He then asked me to love him in the same way, unconditionally. But I replied, 'Sir, what if I should ever find you less than a Christlike master? Could I still love you in the same way?' My master looked at me sternly. 'I don't want your love,' he said. 'It stinks!'"

"I understand, Sir," I assured him. He had struck at the heart of my greatest weakness: intellectual doubt. With deep feeling I said to him, "I give you my unconditional love!"

He went on to give me various instructions.

"Now, then, come kneel before me."

I did so. He made me repeat, in the name of God,

Jesus Christ, and our line of gurus, the vows of discipleship and of renunciation.

Next he placed the forefinger of his right hand on my chest, over the heart. For at least two minutes his arm vibrated, almost violently. Incredibly, from that moment onward, my consciousness, in some all-penetrating manner, was transformed.

I left his interview room in a daze. Norman, on hearing the news of my acceptance, embraced me lovingly. It was unusual, to say the least, for a disciple to be accepted so soon. A few moments later, Master came out from behind the open curtain on the lecture platform. Smiling at us quietly, he said:

"We have a new brother."

A Selection of Other Books by J. Donald Walters

Cities of Light — What Communities Can Accomplish, and the Need for Them in Our Times.

Crises in Modern Thought — Solutions to the Problems of Meaninglessness. This book probes the discoveries of modern science for their pertinence to lasting human values.

The Artist as a Channel — a book that proposes a new approach to the Arts, one that combines deep, intuitive feeling with clear and meaningful insight.

Rays of the Same Light — Parallel Passages, with Commentary, from the Bible and the Bhagavad Gita.

The Art of Supportive Leadership — a practical handbook for people in positions of responsibility.

Education for Life — a book on childhood education.

The Story of Crystal Hermitage — the building of a home, and a life.

How To Be a Channel — how to truly transmit inspiration received from sources other than the ego.

Secrets of Happiness — daily thoughts for the month.

Affirmations & Prayers — a collection of 52 spiritual qualities and a discussion of each, with an affirmation and prayer for its realization.

The Land of Golden Sunshine — a poetic parable.

On Wings of Joy — songs and poems of Divine Joy.

Ring,Bluebell,Ring! — songs and poems for children.

J. Donald Walters resides at Ananda World Brotherhood Village, the spiritual community he founded in 1968. Ananda is one of the most successful intentional communities in the world. For further information about the community, its guest programs, or a product brochure, please write the publisher, or call 916-292-3065.